TACO MEGAREGION
THE ESSENTIAL GUIDE TO SAN DIEGO & TIJUANA'S BEST TACOS

W. SCOTT KOENIG

Foreword: Antonio Ley (El Tony Tee)
Editor: Nicholas Gilman

Taco Megaregion
The Essential Guide to San Diego & Tijuana's Best Tacos

© Copyright 2024 Koenig Creative LLC. All content, photos and illustrations are the copyright of Koenig Creative LLC unless otherwise stated.

By: W. Scott Koenig
www.AGringoInMexico.com
Scott@AGringoInMexico.com

Social Media: Facebook/Instagram/YouTube/TikTok: @agringoinmexico

Foreword by: Antonio Ley
Chula Vista, California

Editor: Nicholas Gilman
www.GoodFoodMexico.com
Mexico City, Mexico

Cover photo: Campechano taco of carne asada and adobada at Tacos El Rey, Tijuana

Trade Paperback ISBN: 978-1-7321020-3-3
eBook ISBN: 978-1-7321020-4-0

All rights reserved. No part of this publication may be reproduced, stored in a retrieval system or transmitted in any form or by any means, electronic, mechanical, photocopying, recording or otherwise, without the prior permission of the publisher and/or author.

Menus, prices, locations, hours and operating status of the establishments listed herein are subject to change at any time. Although the author has made every effort to ensure that the information in this book was correct at press time and while this publication is designed to provide accurate information in regard to the subject matter covered, the author and publisher assume no responsibility for errors, inaccuracies, omissions or any other inconsistencies herein and hereby disclaim any liability to any party for any loss, damage or disruption caused by errors or omissions, whether such errors or omissions result from negligence, accident or any other cause.

San Diego, California USA

DEDICATION

To Fernando Cuevas. My friend, our partner in Three Amigos Taco Tours, family man and one of Baja California's pioneering tour promoters. Wherever in the cosmos you are amigo, I hope there are good tacos.

ACKNOWLEDGMENTS

Gracias to my friend, mentor and editor Nicholas Gilman. His invaluable book *Mexico City's Best Tacos* inspired me to write *Taco Megaregion*. His firm, always-hilarious guidance has helped make me a better writer.

Thanks to Francisco "Paco" Perez, owner of Chula Vista restaurant Aqui es Texcoco, one third of our Three Amigos Taco Tours and guest on *Tacos with Muchachos*—a segment of the YouTube show *Baja Window to the South* which I hosted. "Taco Paco" turned me on to many of his favorite TJ taquerias, most off the beaten gringo taco trail. And of course, to Fernando Cuevas, the other third of Three Amigos Taco Tours to whom this book is dedicated.

To all my cross-border amigos who took me to feast at their favorite Tijuana taquerias. Particularly my *compas* Julio Cesar Marruffo, Fernando Gaxiola and Ana Laura Holguin—whose advice, "I don't know those tacos" taught me to only eat at those taquerias recommended by friends or with a long line of hungry locals.

To Antonio Ley (Tony Tee), chef Mario Medina and chef Denise Roa, who also guested on *Tacos with Muchachos* and showed me their favorite tacos in Tijuana, Rosarito and Tecate, respectively. Also, to my friend Ramon Toledo, who produces *Baja Window to the South* and—as publisher of SanDiegoRed.com—was responsible for some of my earliest food writing gigs.

To my wife, "Gringo Uber" and San Diego taco co-conspirator Ursula, who accompanied me on a quest to find her native city's best tacos. It's been a delicious ride. And to my son Wolfgang, who recorded most of my *1-Minute Taco Reviews* which appeared on Instagram Reels and TikTok.

Thanks to *"El Jefe"* Jeffrey Merrihue, Xtreme Foodies founder, global gourmand and friend. His insistence that I coordinate a series of Tijuana taco tours pushed me to find only those taquerias that would live up to his unrelenting quest for Mexico's most EPIC tacos.

To Anthony Bourdain, whose adventurous spirit inspired me—and many others—to seek out exceptional street food and drop any preconceived notions I may have had about said endeavor. I wish we could have continued our online discussion about Mexico in person over a cold *cheve*.

And finally, to all the taqueria owners, taqueros and chefs who have committed their lives to preparing one of Mexico's finest *antojitos* and inarguably one of the U.S.'s favorite international dishes—the taco.

SAN DIEGO

TIJUANA

The Taco Megaregion of San Diego, California, U.S.A. and Tijuana, Baja California, Mexico

CONTENTS

ACKNOWLEDGMENTS IV
FOREWORD XI
INTRODUCTION XII
SAN DIEGO 1
   SAN DIEGO/CENTRAL 4
      1. Blue Water Seafood 6
      2. Brujas Cocina 6
      3. El Borrego Restaurant 6
      4. El Comal 9
      5. El Viejón Seafood 9
      6. Fish Guts 9
      7. Fuego Marino 10
      8. Kiko's Place Seafood 10
      9. La Corriente 10
      10. La Fachada 14
      11. Las Cuatro Milpas 14
      12. Lola 55 14
      What Makes a Great Taco? The Holy Trinity 15
      13. Mike's Red Tacos 19
      14. Mitch's Seafood 19
      15. Oscar's Mexican Seafood 19
      16. Steak & Bones Tacos 20
      17. Super Cocina 20
      18. Tacos del Barrio 20
      19. Tacos el Flaco 22
      Street Tacos in San Diego: Pop-Up Culture 22
      20. Tacos El Paisa 23
   SAN DIEGO/SOUTH BAY 26
      1. Aqui es Texcoco 28
      2. Birrieria y Menuderia Guadalajara 28
      3. De Cabeza El Único 28
      Tijuana Taquerias in San Diego: No Border Wait Required ... 29
      4. Ed Fernandez Birrieria 31
      5. El Mejor Taco Avapor 31
      6. El Tío Pepe Food Truck 31
      7. La Central 34
      8. Las Ahumaderas 34

9. Mariscos y Birria El Prieto 35
10. Mariscos El Cacho 35
11. SeaTaco 36
12. Taco Machin 36
13. Tacos El Gordo 36
The Bounty of Two Seas: Seafood in the Taco Megaregion 37
14. Tacos Tiajuana 41
15. Tacos Varios la Rosa 41
16. Taqueria Revolución 41
17. Tuétano Taqueria 42
18. Xolotacos Food Truck 43

SAN DIEGO/EAST COUNTY 44
1. 664 TJ Birrieria 46
2. Antojitos Tenampa 46
3. Bad Hombres Good Mexican Food 46
The Cross-Border Journey of Birria de Res 48
4. Birrieria La Loteria 49
5. Carnitas las Michoacánas 49
6. Fish Pit 49
7. La Mesita Mexican Food 52
9. Mr. Birria 52
9. Taco Azul 52
Beyond the Taco: Other Taqueria Orders 54
10. Tacos El Gallo 54
11. Tacos El Niño Santana 55

SAN DIEGO/NORTH COUNTY 56
1. Agave Birrieria 58
2. Craft Coast Beer & Tacos 58
3. The Craft Taco at Sova 58
Modern Tacos: Creative Riffs on the Classics 60
4. Death by Tequila 61
5. El Pueblo Mexican Food 61
6. Frida's Tacos 61
7. Los Tacos 64
8. Mi Rancho Market 64
9. Tacos Alex 64
10. Tacos Asadero 68
11. TJ Tacos 69

TIJUANA ... 71

TIJUANA/CENTRAL ... 74

1. Asadero Tecolote ... 77
2. Casa Tian ... 77
3. Cien Años ... 77
4. Emilio's Rica Birria de Cabeza ... 78
5. La Cahua del Yeyo ... 78
6. La Especial ... 78

Tackling Tijuana: Travel and Taco Strategies ... 79

7. La Oaxaqueña ... 80
8. La Querencia Baja Med ... 80
9. Las Tres Salsas ... 81
10. Los Legendarios Tacos a Vapor ... 81
11. Satabu ... 83
12. Tacongo ... 83
13. Tacos Al Pastor El Meño ... 83
14. Tacos Chuy ... 84
15. Tacos de Birria del Rio ... 84
16. Tacos de Birria El Sabroso ... 84

Beyond the Tortilla: The Role of Taco Sides ... 85

17. Tacos de Birria Martin ... 88
18. Tacos de Vapor El Güero ... 89
19. Tacos del Koshy ... 91
20. Tacos Don Esteban ... 91
21. Tacos El Franc ... 91
22. Tacos El Rey ... 94
23. Tacos El Vaquero ... 94
24. Tacos Fitos ... 94
25. Tacos Los Paisas ... 97
26. Tacos Los Perrones ... 97
27. Tacos Mike ... 97
28. Tijuanazo ... 98

Embracing Entomophagy: Insect Tacos ... 98

29. Tras Horizonte ... 99

TIJUANA/EAST ... 100

1. Aqui es Texcoco ... 102
2. Birria "Si" ... 102
3. La Carreta Taco Shop ... 102

The Legend of the Baja California Style Fish Taco 104
4. La Única de Culiacán 105
5. Mariscos D'Tocho 105
6. Mariscos El Angel 105
7. Mariscos El Mazateño 106
8. Mariscos y Cahuamanta Obregón 106
9. Taco-n-Todo 106
La Libertad: Timeless Tacos in Tijuana's Oldest Neighborhood 108
10. Tacos de Cabeza (sin nombre) 108
11. Tacos El Dorado 109
12. Tacos El Gallito 110
13. Tacos El Primo 110
14. Xolotacos 110

TIJUANA/SOUTH 112
1. Carnitas El Tío Pepe 114
2. Carnitas Mr. Buches 114
3. Carreta Los Compadres 114
4. Erizo 117
5. Mariscos Los Cangrejos 117
6. Mariscos Walter 117
7. Tacos Alicia 118
8. Tacos de Birria Buchito 118
9. Tacos El Poblano 118
10. Tacos La Pasadita de la 20 122
11. Tacos Salseados 123

TIJUANA/WEST 124
1. Mariscos Ruben's y Charlie's 126
2. Mariscos Tito's 126
3. Mr. Pollo Tacos de Pollo 126
4. Tacos Aaron 131
5. Tacos El Che 131
6. Tacos El Francés 131

GLOSSARY 134
ABOUT THE AUTHOR 142
ALSO BY W. SCOTT KOENIG 143

Antonio Ley (El Tony Tee) at Tacos Don Esteban, Tijuana

FOREWORD

"¡Con todo compa!"

To hear this phrase beautifully uttered by connoisseurs of the Taco Megaregion—the Southern California borderlands of San Diego and Tijuana—means more likely than not, you're at a good spot. The *taquero* will leave this part of your interaction for last, if not previously confirmed by the customer, by asking *"¿Con todo?"* (With everything?). And he does this in front of other patrons, putting all the pressure on you. Reply *"Con todo compa"*, or simply put on a serious face while making eye contact with the taquero and nod in the affirmative. If you don't hear this phrase being passionately repeated at whatever *taqueria* you might find yourself—particularly on the San Diego side of the Megaregion—leave immediately. This is essential taco foreplay before consumption and necessary for proper engagement.

The Taco Megaregion has it all. San Diego and Tijuana mirror and contrast each other in a constant, ever-changing hodgepodge of ideas, culture clashes and mass migration. It's home to migrants from all over Mexico, making its culture and gastronomy rich, diverse and abundant with the flavors and styles of nearly every region of Mexico. The Megaregion is the most expensive place to live in on either side of the border. Both cities can also most likely boast that they have the best tacos in their respective region or country.

Compa gringo Scott se la rifó machín en armar esta lista esencial para taquear en la Megaregión fronteriza. Visiting over 100 cross-border taquerias requires dedication and perseverance that's quite commendable. And it shows that Koenig's a man willing to get out there and search for handheld bites of heaven, no matter where it takes him.

Ideas, culture, food, music and the customs and culture of people will never be abated by walls or political ideology. At this defining moment in history, it's important to celebrate those things that unite people—common denominators and bipartisan areas of agreement. Look no further than the taco for something that brings people together unanimously.

Koenig gets it. *Gracias pinche compa. ¡Andas con todo!*

Antonio Ley (El Tony Tee)
Anthony Bourdain's Tijuana Fixer on "No Reservations",
Corazón de Torta Food Truck

Tacos el Gallito, Tijuana

INTRODUCTION

Along the sunny shores of San Diego and the vibrant streets of Tijuana lies the dynamic "Megaregion", a pulsating fusion of cultures, experiences and flavors. This borderland mecca defies conventional boundaries, seamlessly blending American efficiency with Mexican affability. It's the cross-pollination of traditions and lifestyles that makes this region unique. Nowhere is this more evident than in the tantalizing world of cross-border tacos. Here, culinary boundaries blur as carne asada sizzles and fish tacos are elevated to an art form. From street stands to trendy eateries, the taco culture of the San Diego-Tijuana Megaregion embodies the spirit of unity and collaboration, reminding us that great food knows no borders.

In the vibrant tapestry of the Taco Megaregion, three titans reign supreme: the Baja-style fried fish taco, flavorful tacos of *birria de res* (spiced and stewed beef) and succulent carne asada. As San Diego and Baja California share the Pacific Ocean as a western boundary and the Baja peninsula's eastern coast embraces the Sea of Cortez, tacos of local seafood are a culinary cornerstone. Birria de res, a derivative of the original goat stew from the Mexican state of Jalisco, adds a rich layer to the regional gastronomy. Carne asada can be found on nearly every street corner in Tijuana and is a staple of San Diego's taco shops; it's so ubiquitous, that at San Diego parks during weekends and holidays, the heavenly aroma of searing meat wafts from the grills of Mexican families.

Since moving to San Diego in 1994, I've been on a journey through the Taco Megaregion, absorbing its flavors and traditions. As an Ohio boy weaned on "Old El Paso Taco Kit" tacos of bland ground beef, wilted lettuce and rubbery shredded cheddar—all slathered in "mild taco sauce" and unceremoniously served in a "taco shell"—I'm making up for lost time. I've chronicled my explorations at agringoinmexico.com, on my social media and as host of the YouTube show, *Tacos with Muchachos*. With Three Amigos Taco Tours, I've guided tours of Tijuana with Paco Perez, owner of Aqui es Texcoco in Chula Vista, and Fernando Cuevas of Tours in Baja. We've led filmed tours for Netflix, The Culinary Institute of America and YouTuber Mark Wiens. Sadly, Fernando passed away in 2023; this book is dedicated to his memory.

For taco lovers, the bi-national Taco Megaregion is a treasure trove of flavor waiting to be explored. Whether one is craving the eclectic taco scene of San Diego, itching to venture into Tijuana for a taste of traditional Mexican tacos, or wants to embark on the ultimate cross-border taco crawl of both cities, this guide includes over a hundred taquerias guaranteed to ignite the taste buds. This isn't a complete guide—there are no "corporate" tacos here—only the taquerias that, in my opinion, are not to be missed. Best of all, most of these gems are proudly family-owned, ensuring that every bite is infused with passion and local tradition.

¡Buen Provecho!
W. Scott Koenig, A Gringo in Mexico

Las Cuatro Milpas, San Diego

SAN DIEGO

The quest for the perfect taco begins in the heartland of Central San Diego, the rustic charm of East County, the chill seaside vibe of North County and, particularly, the flavorful tapestry of the South Bay—where Chula Vista reigns as a beacon of Mexican heritage. Nestled in this border-proximate enclave lies a taco paradise awaiting discovery. Along the urban corridors of Main Street, 3rd Avenue and Broadway, one detects the enticing aroma of tacos from both locally-owned operations and a growing number of Tijuana taquerias that have established a north-of-the-border presence.

Barrio Logan in Central San Diego—a predominantly Mexican community—unveils its own array of taqueria delights, each a testament to time-honored tradition. Further, chef-driven eateries like Lola 55 in downtown San Diego offer a modern take on the classic taco. While San Diego's East and North Counties boast their own taco treasures, the true essence of Mexican culinary artistry thrives in the southern reaches of the county.

San Diego's "taco shop" culture is a rich tradition that could fill an entire book, with its myriad "'berto's" drive-throughs—Alberto's, Rigoberto's, Humberto's and the original Roberto's, which opened in 1964, among others. These spots are beloved by San Diegans, who are fiercely loyal to their neighborhood favorite. Their menus are filled with comforting options: rolled tacos, carne asada fries, tortas and the iconic "California burrito"—a behemoth packed with carne asada, rice, refried beans and French fries. While taco shops hold a special place in the hearts of many, I find that the tacos don't quite compare to those highlighted in this guide, which is why, with a few exceptions, they aren't featured here.

While many taquerias in San Diego—often called America's Finest City—gladly accept debit and credit cards, it's smart to carry some cash for those smaller spots that do it the old-fashioned way.

As one embarks on a savory journey through the diverse neighborhoods of San Diego County, it becomes clear that tacos are not merely a dish, but a cultural phenomenon ingrained in the fabric of the region. Each bite tells a story of tradition and community. Savor the flavors but also celebrate the rich heritage and vibrant spirit that make San Diego's taco scene truly exceptional.

NOTE: Refer to the Glossary at the end of this book to reference unfamiliar Spanish language terms.

Rolled pork tacos, shredded pork and chicken tacos and chorizo with beans at Las Cuatro Milpas, San Diego

SAN DIEGO/CENTRAL

1. Blue Water Seafood
2. Brujas Cocina
3. El Borrego Restaurant
4. El Comal
5. El Viejón Seafood
6. Fish Guts
7. Fuego Marino
8. Kiko's Place Seafood
9. La Corriente
10. La Fachada
11. Las Cuatro Milpas
12. Lola 55
13. Mike's Red Tacos
14. Mitch's Seafood
15. Oscar's Mexican Seafood
16. Steak & Bones Tacos
17. Super Cocina
18. Tacos del Barrio
19. Tacos El Flaco
20. Tacos El Paisa

VIEW ON GOOGLE MAPS

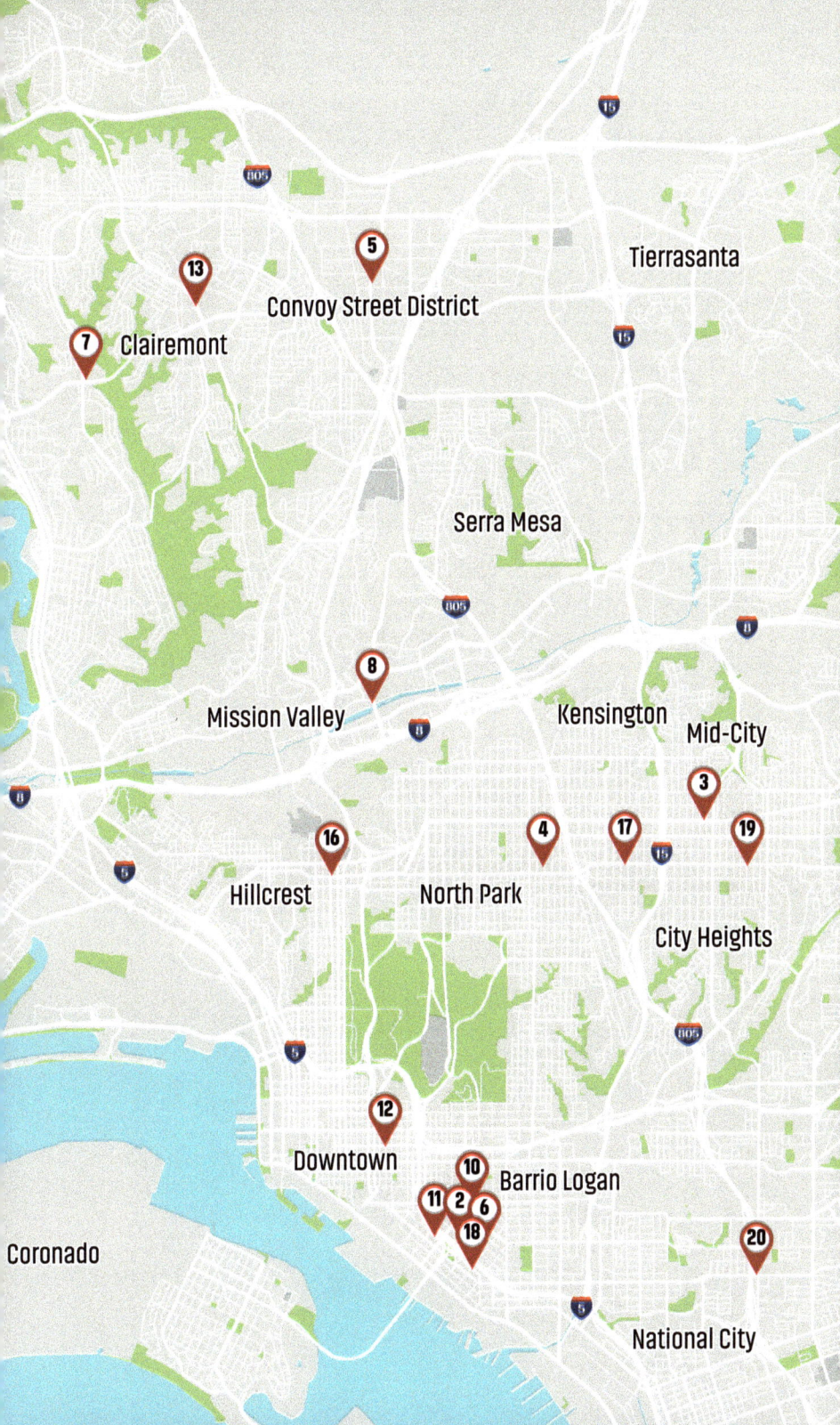

1. Blue Water Seafood

Blue Water Seafood's patio is a laid-back affair—where one can simultaneously savor the bounty and the view of the Pacific. They showcase a variety of local seafood served as soups, sashimi, sandwiches and tacos. Specialties include Baja-style beer-battered cod or the Track Taco with grilled wild Pacific shrimp, chipotle butter and a zesty Maui onion-mango slaw. For purists, the day's catch is available as grilled tacos; think rockfish, yellowtail, seabass and halibut.

SAN DIEGO/CENTRAL

What to order:
Grilled yellowtail taco

Location:
5083 Santa Monica Ave.
Suite 2B
San Diego, CA 92107

Hours:
Sun-Wed: 11:30 a.m. - 8 p.m.
Thu-Sat: 11:30 a.m. - 9 p.m.

Phone:
(619) 255-8497

2. Brujas Cocina

Chef Lety Gonzalez prepares an enticing menu of tacos at her pop-up at Mujeres Brew House. Her Yucatecan-style *cochinita pibil*—shredded pork with *achiote*, sour orange and chiles—is available as a taco or a delectable *torta ahogada*, a "drowned sandwich" bathed in the pibil sauce. The chef's *chile relleno* taco delights; it features a *chile güero* stuffed with soy chorizo, rolled in a round of griddled *queso Chihuahua* and topped with roasted *pepitas* (pumpkin seeds).

What to order:
Cochinita pibil taco or torta

Location:
1983 Julian Ave.
San Diego, CA 92113

Hours:
Tue: 4 p.m. - 9 p.m.
Fri-Sat: 1 p.m. - 9 p.m.

Instagram:
@brujadelacocinasd

3. El Borrego Restaurant

The heart of the Mexican state of Guerrero's culinary traditions are alive and well at this family-owned eatery. Matriarch Rosario Sotelo and her daughter Rodina craft some of San Diego's best *barbacoa*—slow-roasted lamb. Indulge in traditional favorites like homemade *chorizo* (Mexican pork sausage) and cochinita pibil. All-day Mexican breakfast offerings include classics like *chilaquiles* and *huevos rancheros*—eggs bathed in a rich sauce of tomatoes, onions and chiles.

What to order:
Barbacoa tacos

Location:
4280 El Cajon Blvd.
San Diego, CA 92105

Hours:
Daily 8 a.m. - 4 p.m.
Closed Mon

Phone:
(619) 281-1355

Carne asada, portobello in mole and chile relleno tacos at Brujas Cocina, San Diego

Manolarga taco of birria de res and octopus at El Viejón Seafood, San Diego

SAN DIEGO/CENTRAL

4. El Comal

For nearly twenty years, this family-owned eatery in North Park has been delighting diners with a myriad of classic Mexican dishes. Tacos, served on dense, flavorful house-made tortillas, include a sublime cochinita pibil, served with generous morsels of spiced pork. Come for the tacos but stay for dinner and indulge in classics like whole-fried red snapper and *tamales Oaxaqueños*. They also offer several good tequilas and mezcals.

What to order:
Cochinita pibil taco

Location:
3946 Illinois St.
San Diego, CA 92104

Hours:
Mon-Thu: 10 a.m. - 3 p.m.,
5 p.m. - 9 p.m.
Fri: 10 a.m. - 9 p.m.
Sat: 9 a.m. - 9 p.m.
Sun: 9 a.m. - 8 p.m.

Phone:
(619) 294-8292

5. El Viejón Seafood

El Viejón Seafood is a Mexican mariscos mecca amid the dozens of Convoy Street Asian restaurants. The Taco *Manolarga* is heaped with flavorful birria de res and *pulpo*, octopus cooked until tender. It's served *dorado* style with a corn tortilla dipped in its own *consomé* and crisped on the griddle. It's topped with pickled onion, watermelon radish, cilantro and sesame seeds and served with a cup of consomé for the requisite dipping. They have a second location in Otay Ranch, South Bay San Diego.

What to order:
Manolarga taco

Location:
4619 Convoy St.
San Diego, CA 92111

Hours:
Tue-Thu: 9:30 a.m. - 9 p.m.
Fri-Sun: 9 a.m. - 9 p.m.
Closed Mon

Phone:
(858) 737-9192

6. Fish Guts

What makes Fish Guts' tacos truly exceptional are the tortillas made from *nixtamalized* corn—a traditional method that involves soaking corn in an alkaline solution—and use of local seafood. Fish Guts offers an oceanic twist on the classic *al pastor* taco. In this delectable rendition, the pork is replaced with salmon marinated in a luscious blend of *chile guajillo* and achiote and served with morsels of juicy pineapple—infusing it with an irresistible depth of flavor.

What to order:
Salmon al pastor taco

Location:
2222 Logan Ave.
San Diego, CA 92113

Hours:
Wed-Fri: 4 p.m. - 9 p.m.
Sat: 12 p.m. - 9 p.m.
Closed Sun-Tue

Phone:
(619) 888-0081

SAN DIEGO/CENTRAL

7. Fuego Marino

Food truck Fuego Marino delights with seafood tacos, *cocteles*, *aguachiles* and raw Baja California oysters. Tacos are made with locally-sourced fish, grilled or fried to order. The "Melty Gaucho" sandwich is a heavenly combination of grilled octopus, smoked tuna, arugula, avocado and *chimichurri*. It's topped with Monterey jack and provolone cheese and served on sumptuous sandwich bread fried in butter. It's undoubtedly one of the best grilled cheese sandwiches around.

What to order:
Melty Gaucho

Location:
3901 Clairemont Dr.
San Diego, CA 92117

Hours:
Daily: 10 a.m. - 7 p.m.

Phone:
(619) 654-0266

8. Kiko's Place Seafood

San Diego seafood lovers swear by Kiko's for their fish taco fix. Their San Felipe origins in Baja California are legendary—they're credited with inspiring San Diego's Rubio's Fish Tacos chain. The menu is a sampling of local Baja flavors, including their renowned battered and fried fish taco, dressed with *pico de gallo* and *crema*. Some go so far as to claim Kiko's rivals Ensenada for the best fish tacos in the region.

What to order:
Baja-style fish taco

Location:
Corner of Hazard Center Dr. & Mission Center Rd.
San Diego, CA 92108

Hours:
Mon-Tue, Thu, Sat: 10 a.m. - 8 p.m.
Wed: 10 a.m. - 7 p.m.
Fri: 10 a.m. - 10 p.m.
Sun: 10 a.m. - 5 p.m.

Phone:
(619) 341-7397

9. La Corriente

This Tijuana-based seafood haven is renowned for its top-notch raw dishes, grilled entrees and, naturally, tacos. The Kalifornia (sic) taco features plump grilled shrimp and melted queso tucked into a California chile. The Ensenada-style fish taco uses locally-sourced red snapper, a refreshing departure from lower-quality tilapia often used in San Diego taquerias. Order the guajillo chile-battered soft shell crab taco for a deeply-flavorful, satisfyingly-crunchy bite.

What to order:
Soft shell crab taco

Location:
456 Pearl St.
La Jolla, CA 92037

Hours:
Tue-Wed: 11 a.m. - 9 p.m.
Thu-Sat: 11 a.m. - 10 p.m.
Sun: 11 a.m. - 8 p.m.
Closed Mon

Phone:
(858) 203-3132

Soft shell crab taco at
La Corriente, La Jolla

Fish tacos at Fuego Marino Food Truck, San Diego

10. La Fachada

SAN DIEGO/CENTRAL

La Fachada in Sherman Heights specializes in Mexico City-style antojitos. Indulge in capital city specialties like *huaraches* (oblong corn masa cakes) and *sopes* (round corn masa cakes) adorned with one's favorite protein and ample amounts of house-made *queso fresco*. From tender *cabeza*, morsels of beef head, to *adobada*—spiced pork shaved from the spit—the taco selection includes several enticing options.

What to order:
Cabeza taco

Location:
20 25th St.
San Diego, CA 92102

Hours:
Mon-Thu: 7 a.m. - 2 a.m.
Fri-Sat: 7 a.m. - 3 a.m.
Sun: 7 a.m. - 2 a.m.

Phone:
(619) 236-8566

11. Las Cuatro Milpas

Step into San Diego's culinary history at Las Cuatro Milpas, whose *cocineras* have been crafting traditional dishes since 1932. Join the line of anticipatory diners out the door—it's always worth the wait. Feast on a timeless menu of rolled tacos, burritos, tamales and chorizo and rice bowls. A highlight are the signature rolled pork or chicken tacos—topped with fresh lettuce, pico de gallo, *salsa roja* and crumbled *queso cotija*. Grab a pack of their dense, homemade flour tortillas to go.

What to order:
Rolled pork tacos

Location:
1857 Logan Ave.
San Diego, CA 92113

Hours:
Mon-Fri: 8:30 a.m. - 3 p.m.
Sat: 6 a.m. - 3 p.m.
Closed Sun
Cash only

Phone:
(619) 234-4460

12. Lola 55

Lola 55 offers a spectrum of chef-crafted tacos in a chic, minimalist setting. From sizzling ribeye carne asada to smoky, achiote-rubbed pork belly, every bite is an exploration in ingredients and flavor. The bar boasts a fine mezcal and tequila selection to complement the food. Vegans won't feel left out with options like a beet-infused soy chorizo taco. They have a second location in Carlsbad, North County San Diego.

What to order:
Achiote pork belly taco

Location:
Idea1 Apartments
1290 F St.
San Diego, CA 92101

Hours:
Tue-Thu: 11 a.m. - 9 p.m.
Fri-Sat: 11 a.m. - 10 p.m.
Sun: 11 a.m. - 9 p.m.
Closed Mon

Phone:
(619) 542-9155

What Makes a Great Taco? The Holy Trinity

Suadero taco with salsa roja, onions and cilantro at Tacos el Gallito, Tijuana

There are three pillars that form the foundation and success of any taco: the tortilla, the filling and the salsa. Each component is vital, carrying with it a history, a tradition and a flavor that together craft the perfect bite.

Not to be underestimated, the tortilla is the canvas on which the rest of the taco is painted and a culinary staple of pre-Hispanic culture. In Mexico, tortillas are more than just a vessel; they are a symbol of the country's soul and agricultural heritage. Traditionally made from nixtamalized corn, which is corn soaked in an alkaline solution and then ground into masa, tortillas boast a distinctively earthy flavor and a textural mouthfeel. Flour tortillas, popular in northern Mexico and the Taco Megaregion, offer a softer, more pliable alternative. Both types, when freshly made and toasted on a *plancha* (griddle) or *comal*, are the cornerstone of any respectable taco.

The diversity of taco fillings is as vast as the landscapes of Mexico itself. From succulent carnitas slow cooked to tender perfection, to the smoky allure of carne asada grilled over an open flame, to the oceanic freshness of fish tacos straight from the Megaregion's shores, each tells a story. Even vegetarian options, like the savory richness of mushroom tacos or the zesty punch of nopales, showcase the versatility of the taco. The filling is the heart of the taco, providing texture, flavor and substance.

Think of salsa as the soul of the taco, bringing the entire ensemble to life in a wide variety of vibrant hues and rich flavors. Whether it's a fiery red salsa made with roasted tomatoes and *chiles de árbol*, a tangy green *tomatillo* salsa spiked with jalapeño, or the delicate balance of a mango-habanero blend, each spoonful adds a layer of complexity. Salsas can be smoky, sweet, tangy or blisteringly hot, and the choice often depends on personal preference and regional influences.

Tacos, sides and craft cocktails at Lola 55, San Diego

Tuétano (bone marrow) in chile oil with quesabirria tacos at Mike's Red Tacos, San Diego

SAN DIEGO/CENTRAL

13. Mike's Red Tacos

Mike's Red Tacos satisfies with birria de res in all its glorious forms. This taqueria offers specials where one can enjoy two birria de res tacos or *quesabirria* paired with a cup of savory consomé and a side of crispy tortilla chips. The house-made salsas here are very good and infused with a profound depth of flavor. For a unique twist, order a side of bone marrow and scrape the unctuous, chile oil-infused contents onto your taco. There's a second location in Point Loma.

What to order:
Quesabirria tacos with a side of bone marrow

Location:
Liberty Park Plaza
4310 Genesee Ave.
San Diego, CA 92117

Hours:
Sun-Thu: 11 a.m. - 9:30 p.m.
Fri-Sat: 11 a.m. - 10:30 p.m.

Phone:
(858) 737-4299

14. Mitch's Seafood

At this seafood hotspot, tacos are just the tip of the iceberg. An expansive chalkboard menu boasts a bounty of oceanic delights—ceviche, shellfish, fish sandwiches and more. But what sets the tacos apart, even in seafood-savvy San Diego, is the use of grilled, locally-sourced fish—including rockfish, yellowtail, red snapper and mahi-mahi. It's best to enjoy one's tacos paired with a San Diego craft brew on Mitch's cozy harbor-side patio.

What to order:
Catch-of-the-day grilled taco

Location:
Fisherman's Landing
1403 Scott St.
San Diego, CA 92106

Hours:
Daily: 8 a.m. - 9 p.m.

Phone:
(619) 222-8787

15. Oscar's Mexican Seafood

Renowned for serving delectable, generously-portioned seafood tacos, this casual Pacific Beach eatery showcases a variety of deep-sea delights. Options include everything from smoked fish to battered and fried shrimp to tender octopus. For meat lovers, there's also an enticing skirt steak taco. All tacos are available on either corn or flour tortillas. With additional locations in North Pacific Beach and Hillcrest, this taco joint is a local favorite worth visiting for a taste of Baja by the beach.

What to order:
Surf & turf taco

Location:
746 Emerald St.
San Diego, CA 92109

Hours:
Sun-Thu: 8 a.m. - 9 p.m.
Fri-Sat: 8 a.m. - 10 p.m.

Phone:
(858)-412-4009

16. Steak & Bones Tacos

At Steak & Bones, the meats used in their Tijuana-inspired tacos are cooked to order. Savor the anticipation—the wait is worth every bite. The Don Sirloin taco boasts a generous cut of steak, grilled and served atop a house-made flour tortilla. For a flavorful twist, try the *Taco Presidente*, a Poblano chile loaded with melted *quesillo* and hearty grilled shrimp. Dress with a selection of homemade salsas and pair with a cold craft beer from Tijuana and San Diego breweries.

SAN DIEGO/CENTRAL

What to order:
Bad to the Bone
(beef rib taco)

Location:
3923 Fourth Ave.
San Diego, CA 92103

Hours:
Thu: 11 a.m. - 9 p.m.
Fri-Sat: 11 a.m. - 9:30 p.m.
Sun: 11 a.m. - 5 p.m.
Closed Mon-Wed

Phone:
(619) 915-6992

17. Super Cocina

Explore the vibrant heart of Mexico with Super Cocina's rotating menu of regional delights. They offer tender Michoacán-style *carnitas*, luscious Jalisco style *birria de chivo*—spiced and stewed goat—and a velvety mole Poblano among the daily offerings. While not necessarily a taqueria, the shredded beef and chicken tacos, served in soft or hard-shell tortillas, are a must-try—or indulge in a plate of *guisados* with a stack of warm, house-made corn tortillas.

What to order:
Shredded chicken taco

Location:
3627 University Ave.
San Diego, CA 92104

Hours:
Mon-Thu: 8:30 a.m. - 8:30 p.m.
Fri-Sun: 8 a.m. - 8:30 p.m.

Phone:
(619) 584-6244

18. Tacos del Barrio

The Mexicali-style tacos at Barrio Logan's Border X Brewing are a delight. They're among the rare taquerias in town that grill their carne asada over wood fire, infusing the meat with a smoky char. The adobada also impresses—the marinade has both tangy and spicy notes. Tacos del Barrio also offers chorizo, chicken and vegan options. Tacos pair well with one of Border X's Mexican-inspired beers, such as the hibiscus flower-infused *saison* or *pepino* (cucumber) and lime sour.

What to order:
Campechano taco of carne asada and chorizo

Location:
2181 Logan Ave.
San Diego, CA 92113

Hours:
Mon-Fri: 4 p.m. - 10 p.m.
Sat-Sun: 12 p.m. - 11 p.m.

Phone:
(858) 405-0528

Don Sirloin taco at Steak & Bones Tacos, San Diego

19. Tacos el Flaco

A family of Tijuana *taqueros* ventures across the border every weekend to serve a taste of their town's true Mexican flavors. This sidewalk pop-up is very popular with in-the-know regulars, for good reason. On offer are TJ-style adobada and carne asada from Friday to Sunday afternoon, and on Sunday morning, some of the most delectable birria de res in the area. El Flaco's guacamole, which graces every carne asada or adobada taco, is blended until lusciously creamy.

What to order:
Adobada and carne asada vampiro

Location:
4601 University Ave.
Corner of University Ave. & 46th St.
San Diego, CA 92105

Hours:
Fri-Sat: 4:30 p.m. - 11 p.m.
Sun: 10 a.m. - 11 p.m.
Cash & Zelle only

Instagram:
@tacos_elflacosd

Street Tacos in San Diego: Pop-Up Culture

Cristina and David of Tacos Varios La Rosa, Chula Vista

Taco pop-ups in San Diego have found a way to straddle the line between legality and innovation. These temporary food stands often partner with established businesses or operate within permitted areas, thus skirting some of the stringent requirements that traditional street vendors face. The allure of pop-ups lies in their ephemeral nature—they bring an element of surprise and exclusivity, often announced via social media, creating a buzz that draws crowds eager for a unique culinary experience.

Take, for example, Tacos Varios La Rosa in Chula Vista. This husband-and-wife-owned enterprise joins forces with Frank's Batteries to offer their delectable tacos *varios* (*guisados*) from a makeshift, canopy-covered kitchen located in the battery shop's parking lot every Saturday and Sunday morning. Their chile relleno, milanesa and other guisados are not to be missed.

20. Tacos El Paisa

The tacos at the charmingly-rustic Tacos El Paisa in National City range from carne asada to more esoteric options like *buche*—gelatinous pork stomach. The savory cabeza taco is piled high with tender morsels of meat. All tacos are served with a platter of house-made salsas—ranging from a zesty salsa verde to a searingly-spicy habanero—as well as fresh limes, cilantro, onions and radishes. Everything one needs to customize their taco to taste.

SAN DIEGO/CENTRAL

What to order:
Cabeza taco

Location:
3096 National Ave.
San Diego, CA 92133

Hours:
Sun-Thu: 9 a.m. - 10 p.m.
Fri-Sat: 9 a.m. - 11 p.m.

Phone:
(619) 231-0622

Another successful street taco vendor is Tacos El Flaco, which appears on the sidewalk at the corner of University & 46th Street every Friday-Sunday where they sell Tijuana-style adobada and carne asada in the afternoon and birria de res Sunday mornings. This operation captures the spirit of street food in Tijuana. In fact, the owners live in the Mexican border city, and like most Tijuanenses, know what makes a great taco.

Yet others work with local breweries to offer a food option. Brujas Cocina, chef Lety Gonzalez's pop-up at Mujeres Brew House in Barrio Logan, is a match made in taco heaven. Lety crafts an irresistible menu of tacos and other antojitos at this Latina-owned craft brewery. One of her chef-crafted, yet steeped in tradition, tacos is the perfect complement to a cold *cerveza* on Mujeres Brew House's outdoor patio.

Despite the legal challenges, the rise of street food vending and pop-ups, especially taco stands, continues unabated. This movement is driven by a community that values good food, tradition and the communal experience that these vendors provide.

Chef Lety Gonzalez of Brujas Cocina, Mujeres Brew House, San Diego

Tacos El Flaco, San Diego

SAN DIEGO/SOUTH BAY

1. Aqui es Texcoco
2. Birrieria y Menuderia Guadalajara
3. De Cabeza El Único
4. Ed Fernandez Birria
5. El Mejor Taco Avapor
6. El Tío Pepe Food Truck
7. La Central
8. Las Ahumaderas
9. Mariscos y Birria El Prieto
10. Mariscos El Cacho
11. SeaTaco
12. Taco Machin
13. Tacos El Gordo
14. Tacos Tiajuana
15. Tacos Varios La Rosa
16. Taqueria Revolución
17. Tuétano Taqueria
18. Xolotacos Food Truck

VIEW ON GOOGLE MAPS

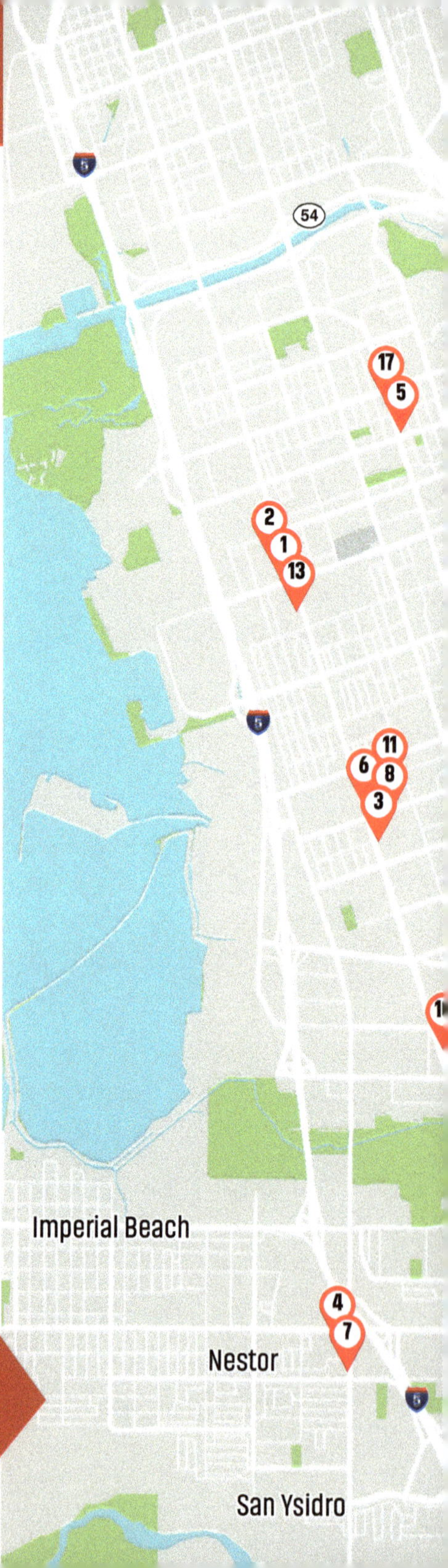

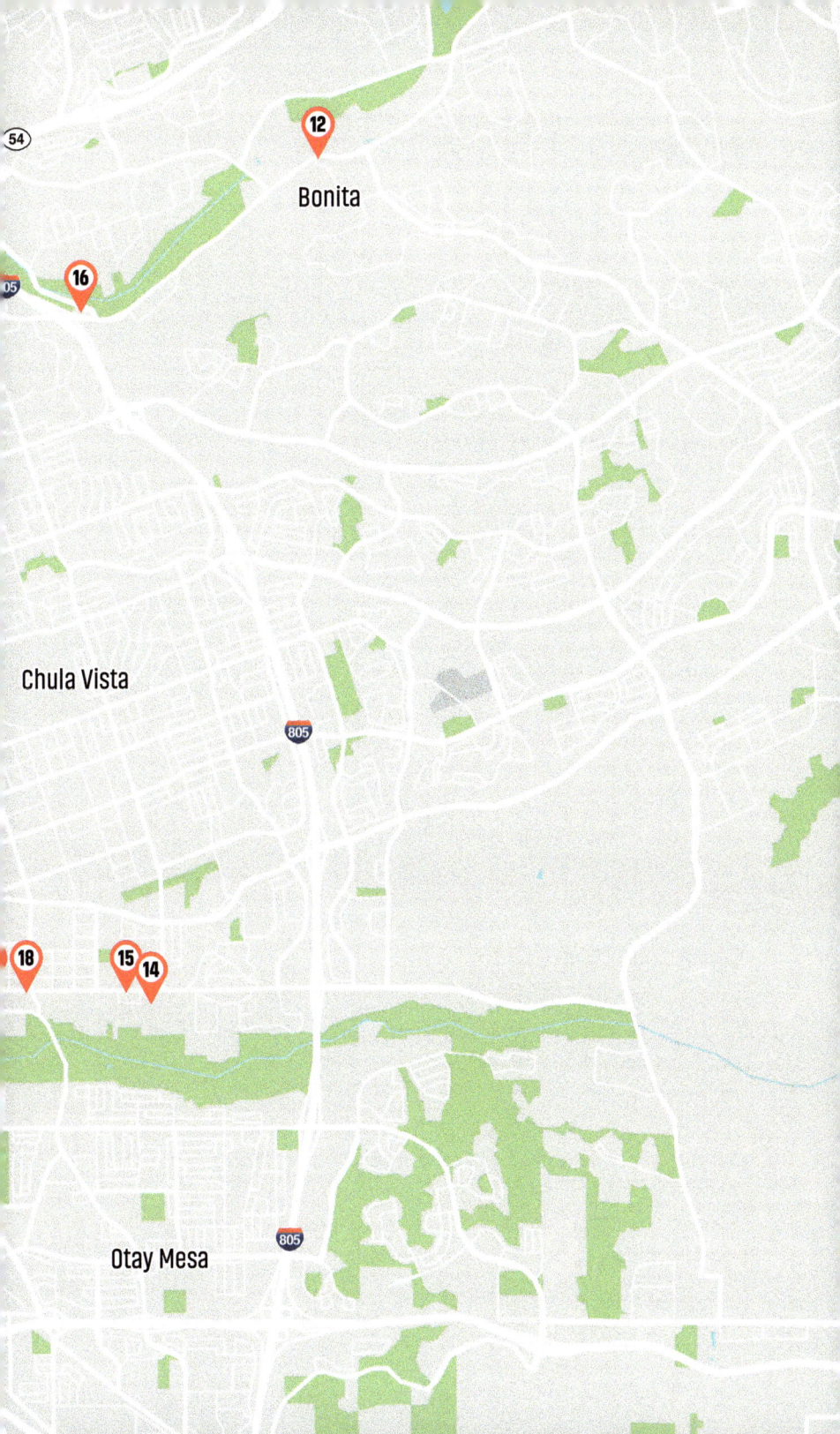

1. Aqui es Texcoco

Aqui es Texcoco specializes in barbacoa of exquisitely-roasted lamb, served with a stack of warm corn tortillas, or as *suave* (soft) or dorado tacos. They're best dressed with the house-made salsa *borracha*—a drunkenly delicious combination of smoky chiles and tequila. For the adventurous eater, the umami-rich *quesotacos*, where a griddled round of cheese replaces the tortilla, can be ordered with *sesos* (brains), *moronga* (blood sausage) or *huitlacoche* (corn fungus).

SAN DIEGO/SOUTH BAY

What to order:
Barbacoa tacos

Location:
520 Broadway 5 & 6
Chula Vista, CA 91910

Hours:
Daily: 9 a.m. - 9 p.m.

Phone:
(619) 427-4045

2. Birrieria y Menuderia Guadalajara

With three locations in San Diego, Birrieria y Menuderia Guadalajara offers some of the best birria de chivo north of the Mexican state of Jalisco. One can order a classic, rich stew of goat on its own with a side of tortillas, as a taco or as quesabirria with melted cheese. They also prepare a very good birria de res which can be combined with fried *tripas*, chicharrones, *lengua* (beef tongue) or *nervio* (tendon) for a delicious taco experience.

What to order:
Birria de chivo quesabirria

Location:
396 Broadway
Chula Vista, CA 91910

Hours:
Daily: 8 a.m. - 4 p.m.

Phone:
(619) 691-1012

3. De Cabeza El Único

De Cabeza El Único specializes in Sinaloa-style cabeza served as a stew or tacos. Other beef head taco choices showcase some truly tantalizing treats—from tender *cachete* (cheek) to *ojos* (eye ligament), to lengua and even *labia* (lips). Tacos, like the scrumptious cochinita pibil and *chorizo verde* (green pork sausage) from Toluca, offer a true taste journey to culinary regions of Mexico seldom found in San Diego's taco scene.

What to order:
Cabeza *surtida* (mixed head meat) taco

Location:
1043 Broadway #108
Chula Vista, CA 91911

Hours:
Daily: 8 a.m. - 9 p.m.

Phone:
(619) 349-2505

Tijuana Taquerias in San Diego: No Border Wait Required

Xolotacos Food Truck, Chula Vista

Tacos El Gordo was the first Tijuana-based taqueria to establish itself in San Diego in 1980. This move introduced Southern Californians to the flavors of Tijuana-style tacos, characterized by grilled and griddled meats garnished with cilantro, onions and guacamole, and typically topped with a spicy salsa of *chile de árbol*. Over the past decade, this trend has grown, with other Tijuana taquerias opening primarily in San Diego's South Bay to cater to the area's largely Mexican community—a testament to the tradition and flavors of their offerings.

Among these culinary pioneers is Xolotacos, with locations in Chula Vista, Imperial Beach and National City. As at their five Tijuana branches, Xolotacos offers birria de res from the same recipe used south of the border. Tacos are served dorado style, where corn tortillas are dipped in consomé and griddled to a crisp.

El Tío Pepe, who hails from Guadalajara, moved to Tijuana in 1993 and began selling *tortas ahogadas*—pork sandwiches on a soft bun drowned in a rich tomato and chile sauce—from a humble street cart. He eventually expanded and opened two restaurants in the city. You can also find Pepe or a member of his family at their truck in Chula Vista, dishing out the same porky goodness that made them a favorite of carnitas-loving Tijuanenses.

Las Ahumaderas, a block-long collective of taquerias in Tijuana's "Taco Alley," expanded to Chula Vista in 2024. The new location mirrors the vibrancy of the original spot, with a lively space decked out in white, black and red, complete with murals celebrating TJ's taco culture. They've even re-created the long counter from Tijuana, where patrons can sit and order directly from the taqueros, capturing the essence of the original experience.

Additionally, Tacos El Gallo, renowned for their classic Tijuana-style tacos, and La Corriente, Tijuana's home of elevated *mariscos* (Mexican-style seafood), have opened locations in El Cajon and La Jolla, respectively. Demonstrating that Tijuana taquerias are a welcome addition to nearly every San Diego neighborhood.

Birria de res tacos at Ed Fernandez Birrieria, Nestor

4. Ed Fernandez Birrieria

Ed Fernandez Birrieria has been serving savory beef stew to South Bay residents for over twenty years. In 2022, they earned national attention when crowned "Best Taco in the U.S." by an aggregate survey on Yelp!. The tacos live up to the hype. The *Quesataco Extremo* is heaped with birria that's been crisped in the oven, then topped with griddled cheese and served on a supple, house-made corn tortilla. Order it with nervio and unctuous beef tendon is added.

5. El Mejor Taco Avapor

El Mejor Taco Avapor is a favorite of late-night revelers along Chula Vista's vibrant Third Avenue. This is one of the few places in San Diego where one will find tacos *a vapor* (steamed). They offer two varieties: beef with potatoes or *chicharrón en salsa roja*. The "mini tacos" are also exceptional and include adobada, carne asada and *suadero*— a smooth cut of beef located near the brisket. This trailer's hours are dependent on street parking availability, so it's wise to call ahead.

6. El Tío Pepe Food Truck

El Tío Pepe moved to Tijuana from Guadalajara in 1993 and began selling tortas ahogadas—carnitas on a bun in red sauce. One can also find Pepe and his family behind the wheel of his food truck in Chula Vista— serving the same porky goodness as they do down south. The *Chavez Especial* taco is crafted of *surtida*, mixed meats, on a warm, house-made corn tortilla and topped with griddled cheese. Order it con todo and guacamole and a zesty pico de gallo are added.

SAN DIEGO/SOUTH BAY

What to order:
Quesataco Extremo

Location:
2265 Flower Ave. D
Nestor, CA 92154

Hours:
Wed-Sun: 6 a.m. - 2 p.m.
Closed Mon & Tue

Phone:
(619) 628-8235

What to order:
Beef with potato
taco de vapor

Location:
289 3rd Ave.
Chula Vista, CA 91910

Hours:
Tue-Wed: 7 p.m. - 11:30 p.m.
Thu: 6 p.m. - 11:30 p.m.
Fri-Sat: 6 p.m. - 2 a.m.
Sun: 5 p.m. - 11:30 p.m.

Phone:
(619) 731-4834

What to order:
Chavez Especial taco

Location:
975 Broadway
Chula Vista, CA 91911

Hours:
Wed-Sun: 9:30 a.m. - 8 p.m.
Closed Mon & Tue

Phone:
(619) 745-9118

El Tío Pepe Food Truck, Chula Vista

Las Ahumaderas, Chula Vista

7. La Central

In 2019, one of the partners at Ed Fernandez Birrieria left the mothership to launch La Central, just a few blocks down the street. Both serve what many consider the best birria de res in San Diego. All types of preparations are on the menu, including *tatemada*, where the birria is crisped in the oven. The *El Commandante* features *birria tatemada* on a crisped tortilla topped with a lightly fried egg. It's a delicious way to start one's day.

What to order:
El Commandante taco

Location:
1290 Hollister St #106
Nestor, CA 92154

Hours:
Daily: 7 a.m. - 2 p.m.

Phone:
(619) 240-3577

8. Las Ahumaderas

Las Ahumaderas was launched in 2023 by two taquerias from the collective of the same name in Tijuana. This lively space also has stalls that offer *elotes*—Mexican style corn—crepes, and a bar where one can enjoy a TJ craft beer. Choose a seat at the long counter in the back and order tacos of adobada, carne asada, tripa, lengua, cabeza and suadero directly from the taqueros. It's the best way to enjoy one's taco fresh and steaming hot.

What to order:
Adobada taco

Location:
1011 Broadway
Chula Vista, CA 91911

Hours:
Sun-Mon: 9 a.m. - 10 p.m.
Tue-Thu: 9 a.m. - 11 p.m.
Fri-Sat: 9 a.m. - 12 a.m.

Phone:
(619) 500-5074

9. Mariscos y Birria El Prieto

At Mariscos y Birria El Prieto, there's something for everyone. The birria de res taco is generously portioned and bursting with flavor. It topped *San Diego Magazine*'s "Best Birria" list in 2020. For seafood lovers, the mariscos menu features cocteles, ceviches and tacos. The Los Cabos taco is a heavenly combination of smoked tuna, grilled shrimp and octopus. They have several locations in San Diego.

What to order:
Los Cabos taco

Location:
3031 Main St #3029
Chula Vista, CA 91911

Hours:
Daily: 7:30 a.m. - 7 p.m.

Phone:
(619) 495-5247

10. Mariscos El Cacho

Mariscos El Cacho is another Tijuana import that's set up shop north of the border. They specialize in seafood tacos and Sinaloa-style mariscos. The *Chula Juana* blue corn tostada consists of meaty morsels of tuna dressed with caramelized onions and avocado crema. The *gobernador*—a grilled shrimp taco with cheese and green bell peppers—is a favorite and comes heaped with a generous portion of seafood.

What to order:
Taco gobernador

Location:
1655 Broadway
Chula Vista, CA 91911

Hours:
Mon-Sat: 9 a.m. - 10 p.m.
Sun: 8 a.m. - 9 p.m.

Phone:
(619) 500-5730

11. SeaTaco

SeaTaco is a nondescript food truck that parks in the same lot as the El Tío Pepe truck. They showcase Sinaloa-style seafood tacos in a variety of combinations that are sure to delight even the most discriminating taco lover. For a sampling of deep-sea favorites, try the *Taco Mariscada*. It's heaped with shrimp, octopus and fried fish and finished with cabbage and avocado. Add crema and salsa for the ultimate seafood feast in a tortilla.

SAN DIEGO/SOUTH BAY

What to order:
Taco Mariscada

Location:
975 Broadway
Chula Vista, CA 91911

Hours:
Tue- Sun: 10 a.m. - 7 p.m.
Closed Mon

Phone:
(619) 253-4389

12. Taco Machin

Taco Machin pays homage to the classic street food of Tijuana and Baja California. They offer an array of delectable options—from carne asada, adobada, tripa and lengua to a rich and flavorful birria de res served with a side of consomé for dipping. The namesake *Taco Machin* is a Sonoran-style taco *perrón* filled with succulent grilled carne asada, *frijoles de olla*, melted queso and guacamole, all wrapped in a sumptuous flour tortilla.

What to order:
Taco Machin

Location:
4228 Bonita Rd.
Bonita, CA, 91902

Hours:
Sun-Thu: 11 a.m. - 9 p.m.
Fri-Sat: 11 a.m. - 10 p.m.

Phone:
(619) 765-2484

13. Tacos El Gordo

Tacos El Gordo, the pioneer who brought Tijuana tacos to San Diego in the eighties, serve TJ-style carne asada, tripas, cabeza and other border town specialties. Ask for "con todo" and the taco is dressed with cilantro, onions and a dollop of velvety guacamole. The adobada, bathed in cilantro crema, is a terrific combination. The Broadway location is the original and one of two in Chula Vista. They opened a third San Diego location downtown in 2022.

What to order:
Adobada taco with cilantro crema

Location:
556 Broadway
Chula Vista, CA 91910

Hours:
Sun-Thu: 10 a.m. - 2 a.m.
Fri-Sat: 10 a.m. - 4 a.m.

Phone:
(619) 271-7222

The Bounty of Two Seas: Seafood in the Taco Megaregion

Taco Mariscada at SeaTaco, Chula Vista

The Taco Megaregion offers a dizzying variety of seafood tacos beyond the famed Baja California-style fish taco. In this coastal area, the influence of Sinaloa and Sonora's culinary traditions meld with the day's catch from the Pacific Ocean and the Sea of Cortez, creating an array of flavors and textures that are nothing short of spectacular.

In San Diego, local taquerias and seafood shacks offer diverse menus that showcase the region's abundant and varied marine life. For example, tacos stuffed with grilled octopus offer a toothsome and smoky delight. Fried or grilled shrimp tacos are another staple, often topped with crisp, shredded cabbage, tangy crema and a splash of lime. The use of locally-sourced fish such as halibut, mahi mahi and yellowtail can be found in the tacos at eateries such as Blue Water Seafood, La Corriente, Fish Pit, Mitch's Seafood, Oscar's Mexican Seafood, Fuego Marino and Fish Guts.

Across the border in Tijuana, the seafood taco experience takes on a distinct, yet equally-compelling character. The city's proximity to both the Pacific Ocean and the Sea of Cortez means that high-quality seafood is always available. Here, Sinaloan influences shine brightly, with *tacos de marlin* (smoked marlin tacos) standing out as a local favorite. These tacos often come packed with a mix of smoked fish, melted cheese and sometimes, a bit of spicy chipotle mayo. Another regional specialty is the taco de *gobernador*, featuring shrimp sautéed with peppers, onions and melted cheese—a true replication of Sinaloa's classic. The *camarón enchilado* is a spicy shrimp taco featuring a robust chile marinade that will leave one reaching for a cold agua fresca or cerveza. Some of the best spots for seafood tacos in Tijuana are Carreta Los Compadres, Casa Tian, La Cahua del Yeyo, Mariscos el Mazateño, Mariscos el Angel, Erizo, Mariscos Tito's and Mariscos Ruben's y Charlie's.

The blending of Sinaloan and Sonoran influences with the catches from nearby waters ensures that seafood tacos in the Taco Megaregion are not just a meal, but also steady business for local commercial fishermen.

Taco Machin, Bonita

Carne asada and adobada tacos at Tacos Tiajuana, Chula Vista

SAN DIEGO/SOUTH BAY

14. Tacos Tiajuana

This truck parked in the driveway of the Hernandez family's home on a Chula Vista side street is as off the beaten taco path as one will find in San Diego. The tacos, mulitas, vampiros and other offerings are on par with their counterparts in Tijuana. Tripas are perfectly fried—not too crispy and not too wet. Adobada from the trompo (spit) and wood fire-grilled carne asada are also superlative. The exceptional, pillowy corn tortillas here are crafted from fresh masa.

What to order:
Carne asada & adobada vampiro

Location:
135 Mace St.
Chula Vista, CA 91911

Hours:
Tue-Sat: 6 p.m. - 10 p.m.
Closed Sun & Mon

Phone:
(619) 769-4106

15. Tacos Varios la Rosa

"*Varios*" is a regional colloquialism for guisados: a variety of taco types that includes *pollo en mole* (chicken in a rich, Mexican sauce), *milanesa de res* (fried beef steak) and chorizo con *papas* (potatoes). A favorite at this husband-and-wife-operated pop-up is the chile relleno taco, where a fried chile stuffed with melted *queso panela* is served atop rice and beans. Have them add chicharrones (fried pork skin) to the chile for the ultimate taco de guisado.

What to order:
Chile relleno taco with chicharrones en salsa roja

Location:
3651 Main St.
Chula Vista, CA 91911

Hours:
Sat: 9 a.m. - 2 p.m.
(or when sold out)
Sun: 10 a.m. - 2 p.m.
(or when sold out)

Instagram:
@tacos_varios_la_rosa

16. Taqueria Revolución

The Tijuana-style tacos at Taqueria Revolución are nearly as good as one will find just south of the border. The adobada is served with a generous drizzle of cilantro crema, a TJ signature. The rich birria de res is served on a tortilla dipped in consomé and griddled until crisped. Order the carne asada "Sonoran style" and it's combined with melted cheese on a flour tortilla. The roasted salsa of three types of habaneros, for heat lovers only, provides a smoky, spicy kick.

What to order:
Sonoran style carne asada taco

Location:
3001 Bonita Rd.
Chula Vista, CA 91910

Hours:
Tue-Sun: 10:30 a.m. - 9 p.m.
Closed Mon

Phone:
(619) 934-9191

17. Tuétano Taqueria

Tuétano Taqueria opened in San Ysidro in 2018 before relocating to Chula Vista's bustling Third Avenue. Chef Priscilla Curiel has crafted a menu of exceptional tacos de guisados—including a velvety taco de *rajas* (mild chile strips in crema)—and stews some of the city's most flavorful birria de res, redolent of bay leaves and cinnamon. For the ultimate experience, pair and top the birria taco with their signature *tuétano* (grilled bone marrow).

What to order:
Birria taco with side of tuétano (bone marrow)

Location:
216 3rd Ave.
Chula Vista 91910

Hours:
Daily: 9 a.m. - 7 p.m.

Xolotacos Food Truck, Chula Vista

18. Xolotacos Food Truck

Several San Diego taquerias come close to replicating the true flavor of Tijuana-style tacos. However, the tacos served at TJ import, food truck Xolotacos, are a nearly perfect match of their south-of-the-border counterparts. Known for birria de res served with a generous bone of tuétano (bone marrow), they specialize in tacos dorados, where the tortilla is dipped in birria consomé and crisped on the griddle.

SAN DIEGO/SOUTH BAY

What to order:
Birria taco with chicharrones

Location:
3189 Main St.
Chula Vista, CA 91911

Hours:
Mon, Fri, Sat: 7 a.m. - 7 p.m.
Tue: 8 a.m. - 7 p.m.
Wed-Thu, Sun: 7 a.m. - 5 p.m.

Phone:
(619) 576-4871

SAN DIEGO/EAST COUNTY

1. 664 TJ Birria
2. Antojitos Tenampa
3. Bad Hombres Good Mexican Food
4. Birrieria La Loteria
5. Carnitas las Michoacánas
6. Fish Pit
7. La Mesita Mexican Food
8. Mr. Birria
9. Taco Azul
10. Tacos El Gallo
11. Tacos El Niño Santana

VIEW ON GOOGLE MAPS

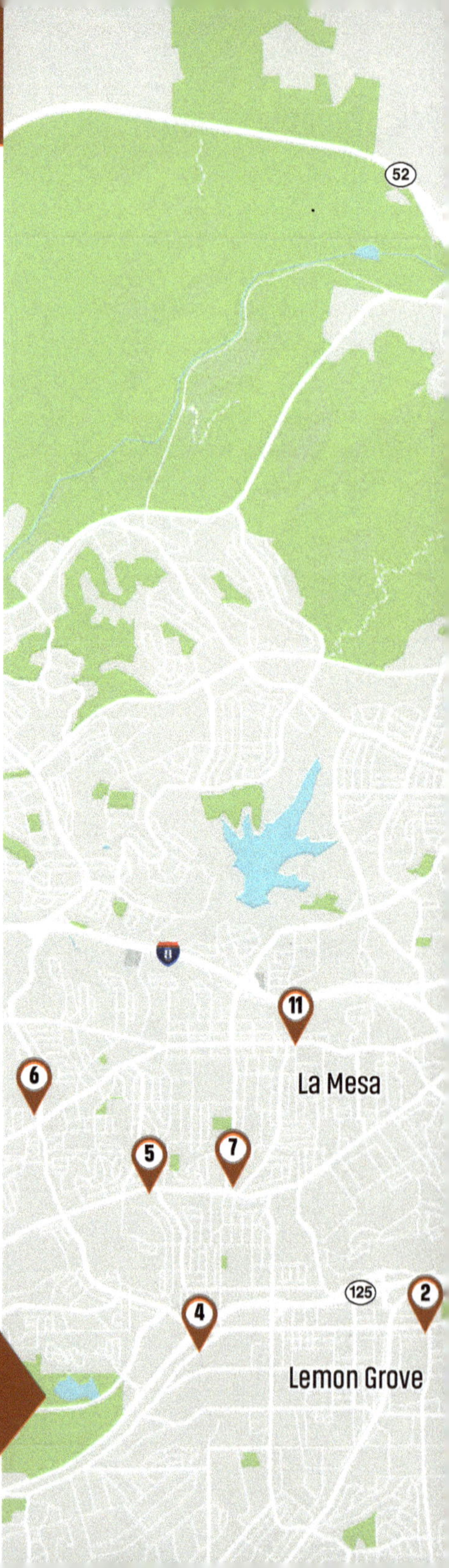

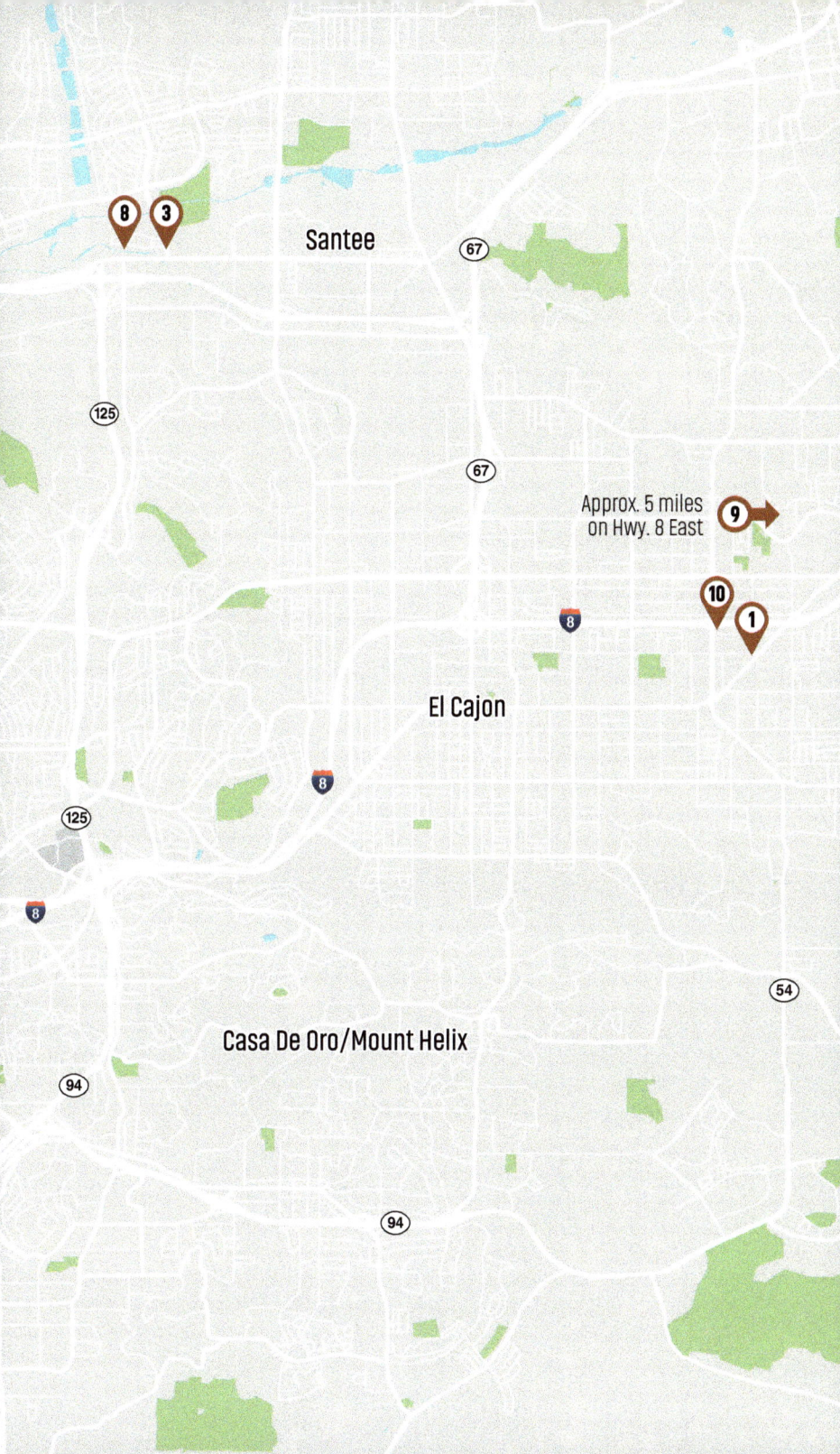

1. 664 TJ Birrieria

SAN DIEGO/EAST COUNTY

With 11 locations throughout San Diego County, this small regional chain prepares birria de res true to their Tijuana roots. Birria is available in several permutations: As an order in a bowl with a side of pliant corn tortillas; as tacos; quesabirria; or with nervio. My favorite is the *Madrazo* taco, which is served with melted cheese on a supple flour tortilla that's dipped in consomé and given a quick fry on the griddle. They also serve menudo daily.

What to order:
Madrazo taco

Location:
1398 E. Main St.
El Cajon, CA 92021

Hours:
Daily: 8:30 a.m. - 7 p.m.

Phone:
(619) 270-7766

2. Antojitos Tenampa

Antojitos Tenampa, a family-owned Mexico City-style taqueria, is tucked into a corner of an older Lemon Grove shopping plaza. They specialize in antojitos—typically corn-based appetizers. The house-made corn tortillas are some of the most flavorful on this side of the border. The campechano taco combines suadero—a smooth cut of beef near the brisket—and chorizo topped with white onion, cilantro and a choice of one of four house-made salsas.

What to order:
Campechano taco of suadero and chorizo

Location:
7977 Broadway
Lemon Grove, CA 91945

Hours:
Daily: 9 a.m. - 9 p.m.

Phone:
(619) 303-4587

3. Bad Hombres Good Mexican Food

Bad Hombres' extensive menu includes classic and "crispy" tacos, as well as burritos, quesadillas and tortas. The "red taco" is quesabirria bathed in consomé and crisped on the griddle. The signature Bad Hombre taco is a take on a Sonoran perrón, a northern style of carne asada taco, where morsels of meaty *arrachera* are heaped onto a flour tortilla and finished with melted cheese, whole beans, cilantro, onion and guacamole.

What to order:
Bad Hombre taco

Location:
8918 Carlton Hills Blvd.
Santee, CA 92071

Hours:
Daily: 8 a.m. - 10 p.m.

Phone:
(619) 938-4454

664 TJ Birrieria, El Cajon

The Cross-Border Journey of Birria de Res

Birria de res taco at Tacos de Birria del Rio, Tijuana

Birria de res, a savory beef stew with roots in the state of Jalisco, has experienced a culinary evolution—one that's led it to the heart of Tijuana, across the *frontera* to Southern California and beyond. The journey of birria de res is a story of adaptation, ingenuity and compelling flavor that has captivated taco lovers on both sides of the border.

Traditionally made with *chivo*, in Tijuana, birria de res emerged as a response to the scarcity of goat in the region. Cooks in the border city, known for their ingenuity, adapted the recipe using beef, which was more readily available and affordable. This adaptation didn't just make do; it thrived.

The rich, hearty flavor of beef melds beautifully with the aromatic blend of chiles, spices and reduced broth, creating a dish that quickly won the hearts and palates of Tijuanenses. The popularity of birria de res in the city can be attributed to its vibrant street food scene. Stalls and small eateries began offering this beefy delight, serving it in warm tortillas—often given a dip in the consomé and fried on the griddle until crisped. TJ's best birria can be found at Tacos de Birria del Rio, Tacos Fitos, Tacos de Birria Martin, Birria "Si" and Tacos de Birria El Sabroso, among others.

Tijuana's culinary trends eventually make their way across the border and birria de res was no exception. In San Diego, a city with deep Mexican roots and a thriving appreciation for traditional flavors, birria de res found a welcoming home. Food trucks, pop-ups and taquerias began to feature the dish, introducing it to a wider audience. For birria in San Diego, check out Tuétano Taqueria, 664 TJ Birrieria, Birrieria La Loteria, Xolotacos, Ed Fernandez Birrieria, Tacos El Flaco and La Central.

The rise of social media further propelled birria into the spotlight. Instagram and TikTok feeds became flooded with images of tacos dripping with juicy birria and consomé, enticing food enthusiasts from all over. This exposure spurred a birria boom across the U.S. from Los Angeles to New York City—where Birrilandia, a taco truck from Queens, was written up by the NY Times and became an overnight sensation.

4. Birrieria La Loteria

Birrieria La Loteria, family-owned since 2021, has perfected the art of one thing: birria de res. Their signature dish boasts a remarkable depth of flavor, making it a great stop for breakfast or lunch. Don't wait too long to visit, as they often sell out by late afternoon. The options are plenty; one can savor birria in various forms—tacos, quesabirria, tortas, burritos, ramen and even a birria grilled cheese sandwich. They opened a second location in Imperial Beach in 2024 where they also offer mariscos.

SAN DIEGO/EAST COUNTY

What to order:
Birria grilled cheese

Location:
6867 Federal Blvd.
Lemon Grove, CA 91945

Hours:
Daily: 10 a.m. - 8 p.m.
Closed when birria runs out

Phone:
(619) 392-4886

5. Carnitas las Michoacánas

Located in a strip mall, this Rolando carnitas joint transports one to old Michoacán, where the best carnitas in the country are served in the quaint hamlet of Quiroga. In the style of this central Mexican enclave, nearly every part of the pig is on offer: from costillas (beef ribs) to lengua, to buche (belly meat). Ask for *maciza* for lean meat. Carnitas can be ordered by the kilo, as burritos, quesadillas, tortas, enchiladas or tacos.

What to order:
Carnitas taco

Location:
6513 University Ave.
San Diego, CA 92115

Hours:
Mon, Wed-Fri: 8 a.m. - 7 p.m.
Sat-Sun: 7 a.m. - 7 p.m.
Closed Tue
Cash only

Phone:
(619) 229-9574

6. Fish Pit

Fish Pit, located just a few blocks from the San Diego State University campus, is housed in a quirky beach shack crafted from reclaimed materials—with surfboards doubling as tables on their cozy patio. While the sushi and raw dishes are the draw, the seafood tacos are not to be missed. Specials always feature a tempting menu of seafood specialties, like a delectable taco of seared jumbo Baja California scallops and a tantalizing blackened salmon taco.

What to order:
Blackened salmon taco

Location:
4632 College Ave.
San Diego, CA 92115

Hours:
Tue-Thu: 12 p.m. - 9 p.m.
Fri-Sat: 12 p.m. - 10 p.m.
Sun: 12 p.m. - 8 p.m.
Closed Mon

Phone:
(619) 793-9911

Blackened salmon tacos at Fish Pit, San Diego

SAN DIEGO/EAST COUNTY

7. La Mesita Mexican Food

While La Mesita falls solidly into the taco shop category, the tacos are a step up from the typical 'berto's offerings. Order a plate of three or five of the mini tacos for the round trip—they're one of the few San Diego taquerias that let one mix and match taco styles for these specials. The cabeza, adobada, carne asada and lengua are exceptional. Make sure to order one of the house-made aguas frescas with which to wash it all down.

What to order:
Lengua taco

Location:
7012 University Ave.
La Mesa, CA 91942

Hours:
Mon-Sat: 9 a.m. - 8:30 p.m.
Sun: 9 a.m. - 7:30 p.m.

Phone:
(619) 697-4455

9. Mr. Birria

Santee's Mr. Birria specializes in birria de res in a variety of formats: tacos, quesabirria, *sopes* (corn masa cakes), birria grilled cheese and even birria ramen. Other tacos are also very good here. Order the taco box of four tacos to sample them all—birria, cabeza, adobada and carne asada. They have five different aguas frescas on tap from which to choose—from *piña* (pineapple) to lemon and cucumber.

What to order:
Taco box of four tacos

Location:
8926 Carlton Hills Blvd.
Santee, CA 92071

Hours:
Mon-Thu: 9 a.m. - 8 p.m.
Fri-Sun: 9 a.m. - 9 p.m.

Phone:
(619) 328-0058

9. Taco Azul

This family-run taqueria on the eastern edge of El Cajon is worth the journey—particularly for the blue corn tortillas, a north-of-the-border rarity, pressed daily from fresh masa (corn dough). The tacos here are all outstanding, from the surf and turf taco featuring carne asada and a generous portion of shrimp, to the cochinita pibil with shredded pork in achiote and spices. These tacos are complemented by an exceptional selection of house-made salsas.

What to order:
Cochinita pibil blue taco

Location:
14110 Olde Hwy. 80, St. C
El Cajon, CA 92021

Hours:
Mon-Thu: 7 a.m. - 9 p.m.
Fri: 7 a.m. - 10 p.m.
Sat: 8 a.m. - 10 p.m.
Sun: 8 a.m. - 9 p.m.

Phone:
619-486-6768

"Blue" tacos at Taco Azul, El Cajon

Beyond the Taco: Other Taqueria Orders

Tacos are the star attraction at most taquerias. They offer a simple and swift way to enjoy carne asada, adobada, cabeza (beef head) and other delectable fillings. Typically served on a single tortilla, many taquerias opt for two tortillas to support heartier portions. Yet, the taqueria menu often extends well beyond the taco to include several other tempting options.

Vampiros

Vampiro campechano of carne asada and adobada at Tacos El Flaco, San Diego

Named for the wavy, bat-like shape the corn tortilla adopts when heated and crisped, *vampiros* provide a unique twist on the traditional taco. Two snappy tortillas sandwich one's choice of filling—whether it's carne asada, adobada, or a *campechano* (a combination of meats)—and are then topped with melted cheese, often *quesillo* (string cheese from Oaxaca) or Monterey Jack. The crunchy tortillas provide a satisfying counterpoint to the soft filling.

Mulitas

Mulitas are like vampiros but offer a softer texture. The tortillas are heated on the griddle for a shorter time, creating a tender encasement for one's chosen filling and garnish. Think of a mulita as a "taco sandwich," where the contents are enveloped between two soft tortillas and eaten with both hands.

10. Tacos El Gallo

El Cajon's Tacos El Gallo is run by two brothers who own and operate a popular taqueria by the same name in Tijuana. There are far too many excellent TJ-style tacos here to pick just one. A favorite is the taco de tripas, fried until satisfyingly crispy. Order it "con todo" and it's dressed with cilantro, onions and a piquant salsa verde. The taco campechano of carne asada is served as a thin steak with adobada and topped with pinto beans.

What to order:
Campechano taco of carne asada and adobada

Location:
569 N. 2nd St.
El Cajon, CA 92021

Hours:
Mon-Thu: 9:30 a.m. - 9:30 p.m.
Fri-Sun: 9:30 a.m. - 10 p.m.

Phone:
(619) 499-5500

New York strip steak and chorizo burrito at Tacos El Primo, Tijuana

Burritos

Burritos aren't common to central and southern Mexico but are a staple in the northern regions, including Baja California. Wrapped in a flour tortilla, burritos are stuffed with one's choice of ingredients. In San Diego, the burrito takes on a unique twist with the addition of French fries to carne asada, rice and beans, creating the popular "California burrito." In other northern Mexican states, such as Durango, Chihuahua and Sonora, burritos are a simpler affair—typically just the meat and sometimes beans—sans the excessive extras.

Tortas

When hunger calls for substance, the torta—Mexico's answer to the Italian *panino* and a direct descendant of it—stands ready to satisfy. Ingredients are generously packed into a sliced *bolillo*, a soft bun, and typically topped with guacamole, onions, cilantro and more. Many taco stands offer their fillings as a torta instead of a taco.

Torta ahogada at El Tío Pepe Food Truck, San Diego

11. Tacos El Niño Santana

A family from Puebla launched a weekend pop-up in 2022 and have since opened on a permanent basis. The tacos include adobada, carne asada, cabeza and pollo asada—best dressed with one of several house-made salsas, roja or verde. They also offer tamales, burritos, tortas, quesadillas and tostadas. True to their Poblano roots, *champurrado*, a warm, chocolate-based *atole* beverage made of masa, is also on the menu.

What to order:
Cabeza taco

Location:
7287 El Cajon Blvd.
La Mesa, CA 92115

Hours:
Tue-Sun: 11 a.m. - 10 p.m.
Closed Mon

Phone:
(619) 955-1356

SAN DIEGO/NORTH COUNTY

1. Agave Birrieria
2. Craft Coast Beer & Tacos
3. The Craft Taco at Sova
4. Death by Tequila
5. El Pueblo Mexican Food
6. Frida's Tacos
7. Los Tacos
8. Mi Rancho Market
9. Tacos Alex
10. Tacos Asadero
11. TJ Tacos

VIEW ON GOOGLE MAPS

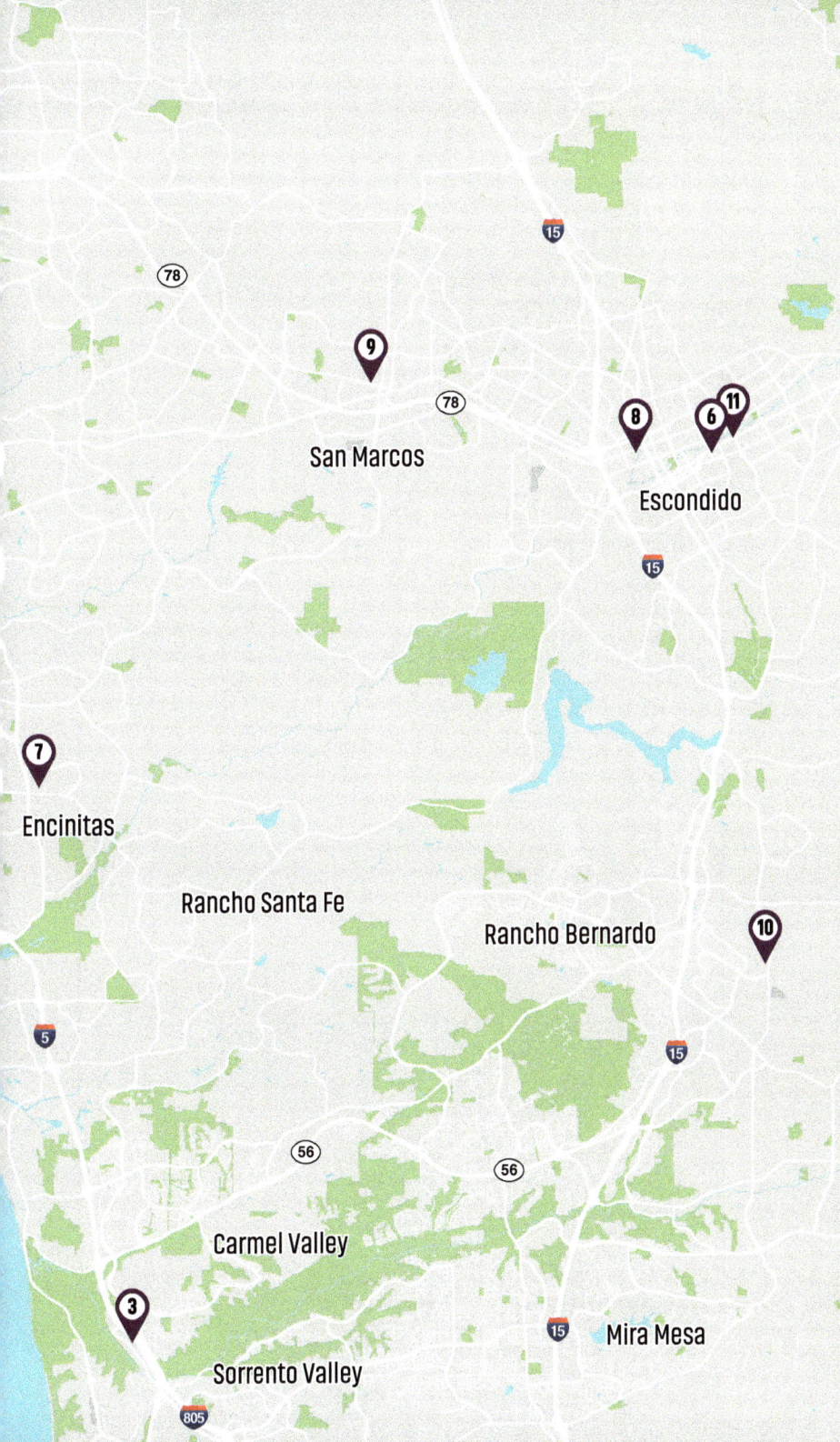

SAN DIEGO/NORTH COUNTY

1. Agave Birrieria

This modern taqueria, adjacent to a gas station off Interstate 5 in Encinitas, surprises with the quality and variety of tacos on offer. The standout here is the savory birria de res, which is some of the best in North County. The quesabirria showcases a generous serving of stewed beef, paired with melted Monterey jack cheese on a tortilla dipped in consomé and lightly griddled. They have a second location in Point Loma.

What to order:
Quesabirria taco

Location:
865 Orpheus Ave.
Encinitas, CA 92024

Hours:
Daily: 7 a.m. - 9 p.m.

Phone:
(760) 452-6228

2. Craft Coast Beer & Tacos

As the name suggests, Craft Coast Beer & Tacos features an impressive selection of award-winning craft brews, along with a tempting menu of Baja-style tacos served on house-made corn tortillas. The carne asada and adobada are expertly prepared. Craving something unique? The mulitas offer a twist, with one's choice of meat nestled between two soft, lightly toasted, house-made tortillas. They have a second location in San Marcos.

What to order:
Adobada mulita

Location:
275 Mission Ave.
Oceanside, CA 92054

Hours:
Mon-Fri: 12 p.m. - 10 p.m.
Sat-Sun: 11 a.m. - 10 p.m.

Phone:
(760) 206-6736

3. The Craft Taco at Sova

The Craft Taco is in a nondescript Sorrento Valley business park adjacent to New English Brewing. They specialize in artistically-plated gourmet tacos. The colossal surf and turf taco combines seasoned grilled Angus steak and plump, meaty shrimp wrapped in a melted round of Oaxacan *quesillo* (string cheese). All this is served atop a deliciously-dense, house-made blue corn tortilla. It's finished with crema, cotija cheese, pickled onions and cilantro.

What to order:
Surf and turf taco

Location:
11585 Sorrento Valley Road
Suite 108
San Diego, CA 92121

Hours:
Mon-Thu: 11 a.m. - 8 p.m.
Fri-Sat: 11 a.m. - 9 p.m.
Sun: 11 a.m. - 5 p.m.

Phone:
(858) 345-1042

Carne asada and birria de res tacos and an adobada mulita at Craft Coast Beer & Tacos, Oceanside

Modern Tacos: Creative Riffs on the Classics

Duroc pork and fish adobado tacos at Death by Tequila, Encinitas

Taco purists, steadfastly loyal to varieties rooted in south-of-the-border traditions, may wrinkle their collective noses at the thought of modern or gourmet tacos. Yet, the rise in popularity of modern tacos—with their inventive, chef-driven twists on classic recipes—is a sign that these embellished creations are here to stay.

The Baja-style fish taco is one example. At Lola 55, with locations in downtown San Diego and Carlsbad, you'll find the catch of the day battered and fried, just like the classic version, but dressed with *remoulade*, chorizo-tomato vinaigrette, *frisée*, pickled serrano and purple basil. These gourmet garnishes replace the typical cabbage, crema and pico de gallo, propelling the taco to Michelin-level sophistication. Lola 55, after all, was recognized with a Michelin Bib Gourmand designation in 2019 and again in 2024.

Death by Tequila in Encinitas opts for simplicity, but with an upgrade in ingredients that elevates their tacos to new culinary heights. The carnitas taco features premium Duroc pork, renowned as the "wagyu" of the pig world for its rich marbling. They also offer innovative options like mushroom barbacoa and grilled fish *adobado* tacos.

Chef Oso Campos, regarded as the Godfather of the modern taco in Tijuana, returned from Michelin-starred European kitchens in 2010 to partner with his brothers and inaugurate the renowned Tacos Kokopelli street cart. He continues to craft these celebrated tacos at restaurant Tras Horizonte. A standout is the Kraken, a taco featuring grilled octopus marinated in Mexican-style pesto and topped with fresh avocado. Pair these with one of their inventive cocktails, such as the *Chapulin Colorado*—a mezcal-based libation blended with prickly pear, lime, bitters and salt infused with toasted grasshoppers.

Chef Jose Alberto Hernandez Garcia presents a tantalizing array of modern tacos at Satabu, his stand at Telefónica Gastro Park in Tijuana. A highlight is the *conejo pibil*, for which the chef meticulously spices, dries, shreds and cooks the rabbit, serving it in a crunchy tortilla shell with avocado, pickled red onion, cilantro, butter lettuce and radishes. Enjoy these creations with a flight of Telefónica's Lyrica craft beers.

4. Death by Tequila

Death by Tequila crafts a selection of elevated tacos that showcase the use of quality ingredients. The carnitas taco highlights confit shoulder of Duroc pork—considered the "wagyu" of the pig world as the meat is valued for its rich marbling. The grilled fish adobado taco features the day's catch, such as yellowtail, in a rich *adobo* with citrus slaw, avocado, lime aioli and *salsa macha*. An *apertivo* of one of their curated selections of tequila is always a good idea.

SAN DIEGO/NORTH COUNTY

What to order:
Barbacoa mushroom taco

Location:
569 S. Coast Hwy 101
Encinitas, CA 92024

Hours:
Tue-Thu: 11 a.m. - 9 p.m.
Fri-Sat: 11 a.m. - 10 p.m.
Sun: 11 a.m. - 5 p.m.
Closed Mon

Phone:
(760) 795-9143

5. El Pueblo Mexican Food

El Pueblo Mexican Food boasts four spots in San Diego's North County, but the original Cardiff location remains a favorite among both local Mexican families and surfers—testament that the food here is both authentic and satisfying. Tacos are generously sized; they don't do the smaller "street tacos" many other places offer. The carne asada and adobada tacos are the stars of the menu. Relax and enjoy the meal on their cozy enclosed patio.

What to order:
Carne asada taco

Location:
820 Birmingham Dr.
Encinitas, CA 92007

Hours:
Open 24 hours
7 days a week

Phone:
(760) 230-1771

6. Frida's Tacos

Frida's Tacos features classics like carne asada, adobada, cabeza and carnitas, and a tangy taco de guisado of *chicharrón en salsa roja* (fried pork skin in red salsa). The menu also boasts California-style burritos, tortas and mulitas, where one's choice of topping is nestled between two sumptuous tostadas and crowned with a generous layer of melted baby Monterey jack cheese. Several house-made aguas frescas are also on offer.

What to order:
Chicharrón en salsa roja taco

Location:
675 E. Valley Pkwy.
Escondido, CA 92025

Hours:
Tue-Thu: 10 a.m. - 11 p.m.
Fri-Sat: 10 a.m. - 12 a.m.
Closed Mon

Phone:
(619) 519-5657

Carne asada, cabeza and chicharrón en salsa roja tacos at Frida's Tacos, Escondido

7. Los Tacos

SAN DIEGO/NORTH COUNTY

Los Tacos is a local chain—with three locations in North County—that's growing for all the right reasons. They offer a variety of tacos, from diablo shrimp to lengua to a vegan soy-based adobada. Tacos are served in supple house-made tortillas—undoubtedly some of the best in North County. The carne asada is expertly seasoned and grilled and their adobada spit is whimsically topped with a "crown" of pineapple stalk. A highlight is the *choriqueso*—a tempting taco of chorizo with melted cheese.

What to order:
Choriqueso taco

Location:
Encinitas Village Square
1450 Encinitas Blvd.
Encinitas, CA 92024

Hours:
Daily: 9 a.m. - 9 p.m.

Phone:
(760) 452-6502

8. Mi Rancho Market

Mi Rancho Market in Escondido offers a taste of popular Mexican dishes, such as chile rellenos and *puerco* (pork) in salsa verde. Street-size tacos include a wide variety of fillings, including some not typically found in San Diego taquerias—like chivo, *borrego* (mutton) and barbacoa de res, a Tex Mex border specialty similar to birria de res. The lengua imparts a smoky flavor and is a local favorite. Grab a pack of sumptuous flour tortillas from the market to take home.

What to order:
Barbacoa de res taco

Location:
649 W. Mission Ave.
Escondido, CA 92025

Hours:
Tue-Fri: 9 a.m. - 9 p.m.
Sat-Sun: 8 a.m. - 9 p.m.
Closed Mon

Phone:
(760) 738-8524

9. Tacos Alex

Tacos Alex, a tiny, nondescript taco shop on the outskirts of San Marcos, isn't about ambiance—it's about the tacos. Here, you can sample a variety of street tacos: carne asada, buche, lengua, cabeza and several others. The adobada is a standout, with a perfect char that imparts a deliciously smoky flavor. Cucumbers in a picante red chile sauce are a surprisingly good side—they're a spicy delight that complement the tacos perfectly.

What to order:
Adobada taco

Location:
250 W. Mission Rd.
San Marcos, CA 92069

Hours:
Daily: 11 a.m. - 10 p.m.

Phone:
(760) 798-7345

Adobada, lengua, carne asada and choriqueso tacos at Los Tacos, Encinitas

Lengua, adobada and suadero tacos at Mi Rancho Market, Escondido

10. Tacos Asadero

The menu at this quaint, colorful taqueria is compact yet formidable and features classic tacos like lengua, adobada, buche, birria de res, tripas and carne asada. Each is outstanding and can be enjoyed as mulitas, tostadas, tortas, burritos or vampiros. The lengua vampiro offers a hearty serving of tender tongue nestled between two crispy corn tortillas. The suadero, rare at San Diego taquerias, is smooth, tender and marinated in lemon, making it a standout choice.

What to order:
Suadero taco

Location:
15721 Bernardo Heights Pkwy.
San Diego, CA 92128

Hours:
Mon-Sat: 11 a.m. - 9 p.m.
Sun: 11 a.m. - 5 p.m.

Phone:
(858) 592-2600

Tacos Asadero, Rancho Bernardo

11. TJ Tacos

TJ Tacos features tacos of suadero, tripas, buche and others in the style of Tijuana—typically finished with guacamole and nestled in a supple corn tortilla. The savory carne asada is a popular choice. Their trompo of adobada is a sight to behold. The humongous spit of meat holds layer upon layer of sliced pork in a marinade so luscious and juicy, it drips down the side and onto the griddle. It's dressed with cilantro crema, just like they do in TJ.

SAN DIEGO/NORTH COUNTY

What to order:
Adobada taco

Location:
802 E. Valley Pkwy.
Escondido, CA 92025

Hours:
Sun-Thu: 10 a.m. - 11 p.m.
Fri-Sat: 10 a.m. - 12 a.m.

Phone:
(760) 294-7511

Tacos La Pasadita de la 20, Tijuana

TIJUANA

Tijuana shares the world's busiest border with San Diego and stands as a vibrant testament to the ingenuity of modern culinary fusion and steadfast tradition. I've had the pleasure of savoring the city's many gastronomic delights and Tijuana tacos have always held a special place in my heart—and on my taste buds.

The story of tacos in Tijuana is one of cross-border influences and local resourcefulness. It's widely believed that the taco made its way to Tijuana during the Mexican Revolution in the early 20th century—when refugees and migrants from various parts of Mexico brought with them their regional culinary traditions. Tijuana began to flourish as a tourist destination in the 1920s, attracting mainland Mexicans as well as visitors from Southern California—from enlisted men in San Diego to Hollywood celebrities such as Charlie Chaplin and Jean Harlow. It was within this environment that the taco evolved.

The birth of the Tijuana-style taco can be traced to the 1960s when a local taquero began making tacos of grilled meat, imbibing it with a smoky, charred flavor, then topping the taco with cilantro, onions and guacamole. Family-owned-and-operated taquerias began sprouting up across the city, each offering their own spin on the beloved taco. From the iconic Tacos El Franc, where the adobada is a celebration of marinated pork, to Tacos Salseados, famed for their claimed invention of the *quesotaco*—each taqueria contributes to the rich tapestry of Tijuana's culinary landscape.

In Tijuana—or TJ as it's often referred to by Megaregion natives—one can taste tacos from nearly every part of Mexico; including birria from Jalisco, carnitas from Michoacán and seafood tacos from Sinaloa and Sonora. Tijuana's taquerias are not just about food; they're social hubs where stories are shared and cultures blend. The open-air grills, the skillful, efficient taqueros, the crowd of anticipatory customers, the tantalizing aroma of sizzling meats and the pots of vibrantly-colored salsas create an atmosphere that is as much about community as it is about cuisine.

Tijuana chef José Figueroa estimates there are nearly 19,000 eateries in the city, the majority being street food vendors. Our list of 60 essential TJ taquerias is merely an *entrada* to one of Mexico's top taco destinations.

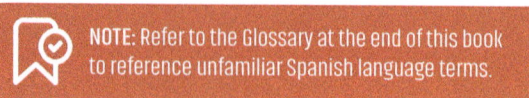
NOTE: Refer to the Glossary at the end of this book to reference unfamiliar Spanish language terms.

La Especial, Tijuana

TIJUANA/CENTRAL

1. Asadero Tecolote
2. Casa Tian
3. Cien Años
4. Emilio's Rica Birria de Cabeza
5. La Cahua del Yeyo
6. La Especial
7. La Oaxaqueña
8. La Querencia Baja Med
9. Las Tres Salsas
10. Los Legendarios Tacos a Vapor
11. Satabu
12. Tacongo
13. Tacos Al Pastor El Meño
14. Tacos Chuy
15. Tacos de Birria del Rio
16. Tacos de Birria El Sabroso
17. Tacos de Birria Martin
18. Tacos de Vapor El Güero
19. Tacos del Koshy
20. Tacos Don Esteban
21. Tacos El Franc
22. Tacos El Rey
23. Tacos El Vaquero
24. Tacos Fitos
25. Tacos Los Paisas
26. Tacos Los Perrones
27. Tacos Mike
28. Tijuanazo
29. Tras Horizonte

VIEW ON GOOGLE MAPS

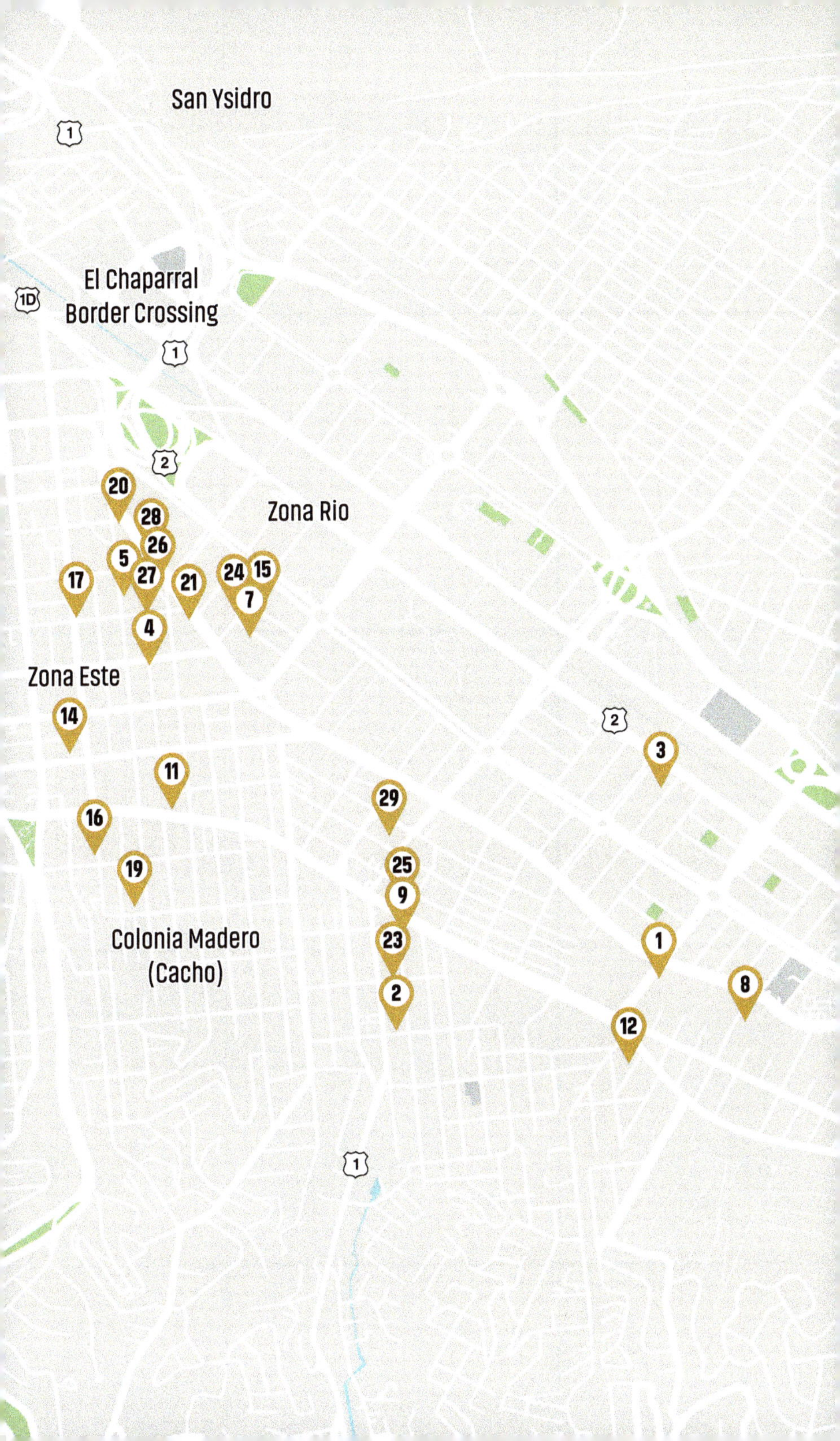

San Ysidro
1
El Chaparral
Border Crossing
1D
1
2
20
28
26
5
27
17
21
24
15
7
4
Zona Rio
Zona Este
14
11
16
19
Colonia Madero
(Cacho)
29
25
9
23
2
2
3
1
8
12
1

Carne asada taco on flour tortilla at Asadero Tecolote, Tijuana

TIJUANA/CENTRAL

1. Asadero Tecolote

Asadero Tecolote specializes in Mexicali-style tacos of marinated and seasoned carne asada. The hefty *Cachanilla* taco consists of morsels of sumptuous grilled beef topped with a round of griddled cheese. It's served on a large flour tortilla—a signature of Mexicali tacos. There's no need to request an order "con todo", there are more than 20 self-serve salsas and garnishes available from which to choose. They have a second location on Avenida Revolución.

What to order:
Cachanilla taco

Location:
Blvd. Gral. Abelardo L. Rodríguez 10385
Zona Rio
22014 Tijuana

Hours:
Mon-Thu: 11 a.m. - 12 a.m.
Fri: 11 a.m. - 1:30 a.m.
Sat: 10 a.m. - 12 a.m.
Sun: 2 p.m. - 10 p.m.

Phone:
+52 663 205 6888

2. Casa Tian

Casa Tian is a chic corner eatery in the upscale colonia La Cacho. Here, one can indulge in plump, sautéed *callo de hacha* (giant scallops) with a squeeze of lime, a dash of sea salt and crushed chile *chiltepín*, along with an array of other raw delights such as aguachiles and ceviches. The outstanding seafood tacos feature a spicy shrimp *enchilado* and a flavorful, crispy *chicharrón de pulpo* (fried octopus) taco topped with pickled cabbage, habaneros and greens.

What to order:
Pulpo chicharrón taco

Location:
Gobernador Lugo 3101-1
Calete
22044 Tijuana

Hours:
Mon: 8 a.m. - 8 p.m.
Wed-Sat: 8 a.m. - 8 p.m.
Sun: 8 a.m. - 7 p.m.
Closed Tue

Phone:
+52 664 900 6438

3. Cien Años

Cien Años is one of the few places in Tijuana where one can order insect tacos. Chef José Sparza serves a variety of bugs atop soft, house-made blue corn tortillas. The seasonal menu offers *chapulines* (grasshoppers), *chicatanas*, (flying ants from Oaxaca), *gusanos* (maguey cactus worms) and my favorite, *escamoles* (ant larvae). The escamoles are combined with onions, jalapeño and garlic and flambéed in butter and mezcal tableside.

What to order:
Escamoles taco

Location:
José María Velazco 2331
Zona Rio
22010 Tijuana

Hours:
Daily: 8 a.m. - 4 p.m.

Phone:
+52 664 634 3039

4. Emilio's Rica Birria de Cabeza

Emilio's Rica Birria de Cabeza—a tiny cart near the border—is not to be missed. In business for nearly thirty years, Emilio stews then rapidly chops succulent morsels of beef head, including the cheek, tongue, palate, lips and sesos and serves them with a side of savory consomé. Make sure to get there the first thing in the morning as Emilio's cart often runs out of *birria de cabeza* by noon.

TIJUANA/CENTRAL

What to order:
Birria de cabeza taco

Location:
Quintana Roo between Calle 10 and Calle 9
Zona Este
22000 Tijuana

Hours:
Daily: 8 a.m. - 12 p.m.
Cash only

5. La Cahua del Yeyo

This unassuming Sonoran-style seafood eatery is a mariscos hotspot. A standout here is the *cahuamanta*, which one can enjoy either as tacos or as a hearty stew, brimming with tender manta ray, plump shrimp and vegetables in a richly-seasoned broth. The Tres Animales taco is a must-try, offering an irresistible mix of manta ray, shrimp and gelatinous *aleta* (tuna fin) that creates an unforgettable blend of textures and flavors.

What to order:
Tres Animales taco

Location:
Calle Sirak Baloyan #1542
22000 Tijuana

Hours:
Mon-Wed: 9 a.m. - 3:30 p.m.
Thu: 9 a.m. - 5 p.m.
Fri-Sun: 9 a.m. - 3:30 p.m.

Phone:
+52 664 638 1156

6. La Especial

La Especial, founded in 1952, is located on the lively Avenida Revolución. It's renowned for its ground beef tacos a vapor. These tacos are piled high, covered with a fresh, damp cloth and steamed until pillowy soft, much like Mexico City's beloved *tacos de canasta*. Each taco comes with crisp radishes, tangy pickled carrots and a fresh spring onion, meant to be enjoyed alongside the taco. For the perfect finishing touch, add a splash of fiery chile de árbol salsa.

What to order:
Ground beef taco a vapor

Location:
Av. Revolución 718
Zona Centro
22000 Tijuana

Hours:
Daily: 10 a.m. - 10 p.m.

Phone:
+52 664 686 6258

Tackling Tijuana: Travel and Taco Strategies

Plaza Santa Cecilia, Tijuana

Navigating Tijuana's frenetic streets and labyrinthine neighborhoods can be a daunting task for the first time visitor—but fear not. One can park on the U.S. side of the border in San Ysidro in one of the many paid lots and cross on foot to embark on a personal taco pilgrimage. With the aid of this guide and your chariot of choice—be it taxi, Uber or Didi—get ready for a taste of tacos at their source.

If driving across, Mexican liability auto insurance is required. There are reputable stateside providers, such as BajaBound.com, DiscoverBaja.com and others, that make it easy to buy a policy online prior to departure.

A passport is required, as is an FMM (Mexican migration form), which can be procured from immigration when entering Tijuana. The FMM is free for a stay in Baja California of seven days or less. For stays of up to 180 days, the fee is typically around $30 U.S., depending on the prevailing exchange rate.

The San Diego-Tijuana border is the busiest in the world. Be prepared when returning to San Diego—even the pedestrian lines can be long during holidays and weekends, particularly Sundays. The Otay Mesa crossing is a viable alternative and often has shorter wait times.

Many taquerias are cash-only; make sure to purchase pesos at one of the several *casas de cambios* (exchange shops) in San Ysidro. Better yet, visit an ATM (*cajero automático*) after crossing the border, where one will usually get the best exchange rate. Most taquerias also accept U.S. dollars.

TJ taquerias keep hours aligned with when their type of tacos are eaten. Birria de res, tacos a vapor and tacos varios (guisados) stands open first thing in the morning and close in the early afternoon. Carne asada is typically consumed in the afternoon, evening, or nighttime, so these taquerias set their hours accordingly.

At the taqueria, review the menu board to see what types of tacos are on offer. If there's no menu, regulars are usually happy to recommend their favorites. For a taco with everything, ask for it "con todo". Order tacos first then grab a drink from the cooler or enjoy an agua fresca (flavored water), if available. In Mexico, it's customary to pay after finished with the meal. Orders are tallied to then paid for with the cashier.

Las Ahumaderas (Taco Alley), Tijuana

7. La Oaxaqueña

La Oaxaqueña, located in Tijuana's colorful Mercado Hidalgo, offers traditional dishes from Oaxaca such as *tlayudas* (corn tortilla "flatbread" with beans, lard, string cheese, tomatoes and meat), tamales Oaxaqueña, a variety of rich moles and an abundance of seasonal insects such as *chinicuiles* (small maguey worms) and chapulines. For a true taste of Oaxaca, try the tacos of *tasajo* or *cecina*—marinated, thinly-pounded, air-dried beef or pork—on a house-made blue corn tortilla.

What to order:
Tasajo taco

Location:
Guadalupe Victoria 9350
Zona Rio
22010 Tijuana

Hours:
Mon-Sat: 7:30 a.m. - 5:30 p.m.
Sun: 7:30 a.m. - 3:30 p.m.

Phone:
+52 664 200 2920

8. La Querencia Baja Med

At chef Miguel Angel Guerrero's Tijuana outpost, Baja Med cuisine takes center stage, blending the flavors of coastal Spain, Asia and Mexico. Expect hearty tacos served on grilled corn tortillas—each a tribute to Guerrero's rustic spirit. Offerings may include seared bluefin, borrego, roasted duck breast and chorizo crafted from local abalone. It's a must-visit for those seeking a true taste of Baja California cuisine.

What to order:
Chorizo *abulón* taco

Location:
Escuadrón 201 No. 3110
Zona Centro
22014 Tijuana

Hours:
Mon-Sat: 1 p.m. - 10 p.m.
Closed Sun

Phone:
+52 664 972 9935

9. Las Tres Salsas

Las Ahumaderas (also known as "Taco Alley"), a block-long collective of taquerias, is open until 5 a.m., making it a popular spot for after-hours taco fanatics. Las Tres Salsas offers a variety of meat-filled tacos such as carne asada, tripa and chorizo. The taquero shaves slice after tender slice of adobada from the spit directly into a waiting warm corn tortilla held in his other hand. Ask for it "con todo" and guacamole, onions, cilantro and a spicy red salsa are added.

What to Order:
Adobada taco

Location:
Av. Guillermo Prieto 2620
Defensores de Baja California
22044 Tijuana

Hours:
Tue-Sun: 9 a.m. - 5 a.m.
Closed Mon

Phone:
+52 664 349 5531

10. Los Legendarios Tacos a Vapor

Los Legendarios lives up to its name. For over sixty years, this family-operated street cart has specialized in tacos a vapor, beloved by generations of Tijuanenses. They offer a steamed taco of smoked marlin, a rare treat difficult to find anywhere else in the city. A popular order is the taco of *deshebrada* and cachete—in which shredded beef in a hearty red salsa comingles with tender beef cheek and is finished with onion, lettuce and tomato.

What to order:
Smoked marlin taco a vapor

Location:
In front of Calimax
Corner of Calle Cristóbal
Colón and 2nd St.
Zona Centro
22000 Tijuana

Hours:
Daily: 8 a.m. - 4:30 p.m.
Cash only

Phone:
+52 664 396 6660

Conejo (rabbit) pibil taco at Satabu, Telefónica Gastro Park, Tijuana

11. Satabu

Telefónica Gastro Park is a vibrant collective of food trucks and stalls offering an eclectic mix of dishes, from smoked sausages to pizza. At Satabu, chef Jose Alberto Hernandez Garcia crafts a delectable array of modern tacos. A standout is the *conejo pibil*. The chef meticulously spices, dries, shreds and cooks the rabbit in a time-intensive process, presenting it in a crunchy tortilla shell dressed with avocado, pickled red onion, cilantro, butter lettuce and radishes.

12. Tacongo

Tacongo offers an array of tacos—carne asada, birria, chorizo and adobada—with a twist. Every taco is crafted entirely from vegan ingredients, with mushrooms taking center stage for most and richly-spiced, stewed *jaca* (jackfruit) replacing the traditional goat or beef in the birria. Tacongo is a vegan taco lover's paradise and might even entice the most devoted carnivores with their deliciously-inventive creations. In 2024, they rolled a food truck into San Diego. Check their Instagram for locations and schedule.

13. Tacos Al Pastor El Meño

This unpretentious street cart, established in 1968, offers just two types of tacos, perfected over time. The cabeza taco boasts savory, tender beef morsels, topped with onion, cilantro and a zesty salsa verde. The go-to for long-time patrons, though, are Meño's celebrated al pastor tacos. Succulent spiced pork is shaved from the spit into a folded corn tortilla and then cooked to a slight char on the griddle. Tacos are finished with guacamole, cilantro and grilled onion.

TIJUANA/CENTRAL

What to order:
Conejo pibil taco

Location:
Telefónica Gastro Park
Blvd. Agua Caliente y
Avenida Sirak Baloyan 8860
Zona Este
22020 Tijuana

Hours:
Daily: 12 p.m. - 10 p.m.

Phone:
+52 664 904 7565

What to order:
Jaca (jackfruit) birria taco

Location:
Calle Orizaba 3003
Neidhart
22020 Tijuana, B.C.

Hours:
Tue-Fri: 1 p.m. - 9 p.m.
Sat: 10 a.m. - 9 p.m.
Sun: 10 a.m. - 6 p.m.
Closed Mon

Phone:
+52 (664) 969 9946

Instagram:
@tacongo.tacongo

What to order:
Al pastor taco

Location:
Bravo 1690
Independencia
22055 Tijuana

Hours:
Mon-Tue: 5:30 a.m. - 9 p.m.
Thu-Sat: 5:30 a.m. - 9 p.m.
Closed Sun & Mon
Cash only

Phone:
+52 664 800 8240

14. Tacos Chuy

Tacos Chuy's towering, smoke-belching chimney is a beacon that can be seen from several blocks away. This street stall is located on the edge of the city's infamous red-light district, Zona Norte, and specializes in savory tacos of carne asada and crispy grilled tripas. Make sure to request one of the large, bulbous, foil-wrapped green onions from the grill—best complemented with a squeeze of lime and a sprinkle of salt.

TIJUANA/CENTRAL

What to order:
Carne asada and tripas taco

Location:
Calle 11 Centro
Zona Norte
22000 Tijuana

Hours:
Mon-Fri: 7 a.m. - 3 p.m.
Sat: 7 a.m. - 2 p.m.
Closed Sun
Cash only

15. Tacos de Birria del Rio

Tacos de Birria del Rio has been elevating birria de res to an art form since 1986. The crowd of regulars in the colorful dining area is testament to the quality of the tacos here, particularly in a city with dozens of options for this Tijuana specialty. What sets the birria here apart is the liberal use of bay leaf, which imparts an aromatic, herbaceous note that enhances its flavor. Perfect for early risers—or hardcore night owls—they open at 4 a.m. weekdays and 2 a.m. weekends.

What to order:
Birria de res taco

Location:
Guadalupe Victoria 20
Zona Rio
22010 Tijuana

Hours:
Mon-Fri: 4 a.m. - 2 p.m.
Sat-Sun: 2 a.m. - 2 p.m.
Cash only

Phone:
+52 664 585 5452

16. Tacos de Birria El Sabroso

Tacos de Birria El Sabroso is one of the few taquerias in Tijuana to offer *birria de lengua*—in which beef tongue is stewed with the same chiles, aromatics and spices used for the birria de res. Both styles of birria are expertly prepared and cooked with a balanced, calculated blend of seasonings, allowing the beef's natural flavor to shine through. Tacos are best finished with one of the popular street cart's three house-made salsas.

What to order:
Birria de lengua taco

Location:
Av. Aguascalientes 2237
Col. Madero (Cacho)
22040 Tijuana

Hours:
Daily: 7 a.m. - 2:15 p.m.
Cash only

Phone:
+52 664 821 7971

Beyond the Tortilla: The Role of Taco Sides

Tacos are more than a meal—they're an experience, a celebration of flavors, textures and traditions that create a symphony on the palate. Ever wondered why taquerias offer lime, radishes, green onions and grilled jalapeños as taco accompaniments? There's a purpose to each, integral to the experience.

Radishes at Tacos de Birria Martin, Tijuana

Limes, or *límones* as they're known south of the border, are a Mexican culinary staple. A squeeze of lime adds more than citrusy tang—it balances the richness of meats like carne asada or carnitas, cutting through the fat and brightening each bite. Lime juice enhances flavors, offering a vivid taste sensation. Some taquerias, particularly in San Diego, opt for lemons—or *límones amarillos*—which deliver a similar zesty kick.

Radishes may seem an afterthought, but they play a crucial role. Cooling and palate-cleansing, they prepare one for the flavor of the next taco. Their crisp texture contrasts with the softness of the tortilla, enhancing each bite and ensuring one reaches for more.

Grilled onions, or *cebollitas*, add another layer. Their sweet, caramelized flavor complements savory fillings, adding complexity and a hint of smokiness. Biting into a taco with grilled onions also provides a satisfying, crunchy counterpoint to the supple tortilla and succulent fillings.

Then there are jalapeños. These chiles, grilled to tame their spiciness, impart a smoky depth to tacos. Whether one prefers a subtle hint of heat or an onslaught of hellfire, they offer a customizable level for spice enthusiasts. Some bite off the tip and squeeze the chile's juice onto their taco, infusing it with a spicy tang. Some taquerias also offer grilled *chiles güeros*—mild, elongated yellow peppers.

Tacos de Birria del Rio, Tijuana

17. Tacos de Birria Martin

One can spot Tacos de Birria Martin's sidewalk tent by the smoke wafting from the griddle and the crowd of eager, hungry patrons. Here, Martin and his speedy team of taqueros efficiently combine rich beef birria with unctuous nervio for one of the city's best tacos of its kind. Ask for the taco "con todo" and cilantro, chopped onion and a spicy house salsa are added. Make sure to grab a couple of fresh radishes from one of the enormous piles of them on the tables.

What to order:
Birria and nervio taco

Location:
C. 8va. Miguel Hidalgo
San Pablo CTM
Melchor Ocampo
22000 Tijuana

Hours:
Daily: 6:30 a.m. - 2 p.m.
Cash only

Phone:
+ 52 664 279 9378

Tacos de Birria Martin, Tijuana

18. Tacos de Vapor El Güero

Tacos de Vapor El Güero has been around since the 1960s and many Tijuanenses fondly recall them as a childhood favorite. Look for the bright red and yellow tent which covers the entire operation. Within, taqueros serve from piles of steamed tacos covered with damp cloths, including carne deshebrada, birria, chicharrones and refried bean and queso tacos. Tacos a vapor are very oily and served steaming hot, so handle with care.

TIJUANA/CENTRAL

What to order:
Chicharrón taco a vapor

Location:
Carrillo Puerto y o Tercera 7093
Zona Centro
22000 Tijuana

Hours:
Daily: 8 a.m. - 6 p.m.
Closed Thu
Cash only

Phone:
+52 664 285 7679

El Che taco at Tacos del Koshy, Tijuana

19. Tacos del Koshy

Tacos del Koshy embodies the essence of a classic Tijuana taqueria, but with an upgraded interior featuring a stone taco bar, vibrant murals and colorfully-painted menus on the walls. Traditional tacos are elevated with inventive twists—like the *Taco Exotico*, which features crispy pork belly and melted cheese. The *El Che* is a standout, showcasing a succulent cut of grilled *picaña* (fatty sirloin tip) drizzled with tangy chimichurri and salsa roja.

TIJUANA/CENTRAL

What to order:
El Che taco

Location:
Colombia 2493
Colonia Madero (Cacho)
22040 Tijuana

Hours:
Mon-Sat: 2 p.m. - 11 p.m.
Closed Sun

Phone:
+52 664 974 8336

20. Tacos Don Esteban

Tacos Don Esteban, in business since 1965, is unique in its use of thinly-sliced New York strip steak—vs. the typical skirt cut—for its succulent carne asada. The well-seasoned, mesquite-grilled meat is set atop a thin layer of refried beans and topped with shredded lettuce and avocado. When choosing garnish, make sure to add a splash of mayo—an unusual yet delicious tradition here.

What to order:
NY strip carne asada taco

Location:
Av. Pio Pico 1230
Zona Centro
22000 Tijuana

Hours:
Daily: 9 a.m. - 9 p.m.
Cash only

Phone:
+52 664 204 7494

21. Tacos El Franc

Tacos El Franc began its life in the 1970s as a humble street cart and has blossomed into Tijuana's most beloved taqueria, earning a Michelin Bib Gourmand award in 2024 for casual dining—one of the first taquerias in Mexico to receive this designation. The recognition is well deserved. The frenetic taqueros craft every type of TJ taco one could crave, from carne asada to tripas, lengua and some of Tijuana's finest adobada. Order just one or two at a time to savor everything they have to offer.

What to order:
Adobada taco

Location:
Boulevard General Rodolfo
Sánchez Taboada 9257
Zona Este
22010 Tijuana

Hours:
Mon-Thu: 4 p.m. - 1 a.m.
Fri-Sat: 3 p.m. - 3 a.m.
Cash only

Phone:
+52 664 330 2499

Tacos El Franc, Tijuana

22. Tacos El Rey

Tacos El Rey, a Tijuana tradition since 1970, is the first stop for many travelers crossing the southern border. From this modest sidewalk kitchen, the tantalizing aroma of wood fire and cooking meat fills the air. Savory slabs of carne asada, ruby red chorizo and meaty rows of tripas are deliciously charbroiled. Unless ordered crispy, tripas are served "wet," delivering a rich, buttery flavor and toothsome texture. The house-made tortillas are warm, pliant and delicious.

TIJUANA/CENTRAL

What to order:
Tripas taco

Location:
Calle Benito Juárez 2da 7472
Zona Centro
22000 Tijuana

Hours:
Daily: 10 a.m. - 2 a.m.

23. Tacos El Vaquero

It's difficult to miss Tacos El Vaquero. Two taqueros, sporting white cowboy hats, busily work the blazing grill, cooking choice cuts of Sonoran beef—ribeye, sirloin, NY strip and an exceptionally-flavorful picaña. Dress the taco with an array of fiery salsas and toppings, or the zesty, herbaceous chimichurri—befitting of this steakhouse-level carne asada. For an authentic Sonoran experience, opt for a flour tortilla instead of corn.

What to order:
Picaña carne asada on a flour tortilla

Location:
Gobernador Ibarra
America
22044 Tijuana

Hours:
Mon-Fri: 7 p.m. - 11:30 p.m.
Closed Sat & Sun
Cash only

Phone:
+52 664 477 5438

24. Tacos Fitos

Located outside the city's colorful Mercado Hidalgo, this popular cart's taqueros are known for their agility. They make a show of tossing a spoonful of consomé across the span of several feet into an awaiting corn tortilla filled with birria de res and fried tripas held in the other hand. The tortillas are lightly toasted on the griddle in the consomé beforehand, giving them a golden appearance and crunchy texture. Top tacos with their searing salsa of chile de árbol.

What to order:
Campechano taco of birria de res and tripas

Location:
Francisco Javier Mina 1695
Zona Rio
22010 Tijuana

Hours:
Daily: 5 a.m. - 1:30 p.m.
Cash only

Tacos El Rey, Tijuana

Chile relleno taco at Tacos Mike, Tijuana

25. Tacos Los Paisas

Las Ahumaderas, fondly dubbed "Taco Alley," features a block-long collective of approximately half a dozen taquerias. Tacos Los Paisas was among Anthony Bourdain's stops when he visited Tijuana in 2011, and it's clear why. The samurai taco, with a choice of adobada or carne asada paired with vibrant chorizo, is a taste sensation. But the real showstopper here is the vampiro: which combines carne asada and chorizo with melted cheese, all nestled between two crispy tostadas.

TIJUANA/CENTRAL

What to order:
Carne asada & chorizo vampiro

Location:
Av. Gobernador Balarezo
America
22044 Tijuana

Hours:
Daily: 9 a.m. - 2 a.m.
Cash only

Phone:
+52 664 369 2616

26. Tacos Los Perrones

The taco perrón is a style from the Mexican state of Sonora. Morsels of grilled arrachera are served on a large, supple house-made flour tortilla and dressed with beans, onions, cilantro, melted Monterey Jack cheese and a dollop of herbaceous guacamole. What makes the tacos here particularly tasty is the bath the beef is given in its own broth before served, keeping the meat moist and infusing the taco with an irresistible savory flavor.

What to order:
Taco perrón

Location:
Blvd. Gral Rodolfo Sánchez Taboada 1511
Zona Centro
22000 Tijuana

Hours:
Daily: Open 24 hours
Cash only

Phone:
+52 664 685 7360

27. Tacos Mike

Tacos Mike in Tijuana's Zona Este neighborhood is crowded with hungry regulars who line up for tacos varios—also known as guisados—an assortment of stewed and cooked vegetables and meats. The massive chile relleno taco features a battered and deep-fried Poblano chile filled with a generous amount of melted Monterey jack cheese. Top it with house-made salsa verde and *nopalitos*, a zesty salad of sliced cactus paddles with tomatoes, cilantro and onions.

What to order:
Milanesa de res with chicharrones taco

Location:
C. 8va. Miguel Hidalgo 8910
Zona Este
22000 Tijuana

Hours:
Mon-Sat: 9 a.m. - 3 p.m.
Closed Sun
Cash only

28. Tijuanazo

Tijuanazo (formerly Taconazo), a popular TJ chain, offers a variety of tacos, burritos and tortas. The tripas are a favorite. Cooked until crispy on the outside and soft in the middle, they're extra flavorful as they absorb the taste of the other meats with which they're fried. Served on warm, just-made corn tortillas, order it "con todo" and onions, cilantro and a piquant salsa verde are added. They have five locations in Tijuana from which to choose and, as of press time, are scheduled to open a San Diego outpost.

What to order:
Tripas taco

Location:
Ca. Hermenegildo Galeana 8442
Zona Este
22000 Tijuana

Hours:
Fri-Sat: 8 a.m. - 3 a.m.
Sun: 8 a.m. - 12 a.m.
Mon-Thu: 8 a.m. - 1 a.m.

Phone:
+52 664 685 9350

Embracing Entomophagy: Insect Tacos

Chapulines (grasshopper) tacos at La Oaxaqueña, Tijuana

In the U.S., many visibly recoil at the mention of edible insects, yet they're consumed daily by over 2 billion people worldwide, primarily in Latin America, Asia and Africa. As the population of the planet continues to grow and grazing areas for livestock diminish, many speculate that entomophagy—the eating of insects—will be key in providing the rest of the world eco-friendly protein in the not-too-distant future.

Edible insects were a mainstay of the Mesoamerican diet and have been consumed in Mexico for centuries. Eating insects remains one of Mexico's most time-honored culinary traditions. Many in the central and southern regions of the country still consume the critters as part of their daily sustenance.

It's common to find baskets of crunchy *chapulines* (fried grasshoppers seasoned with lime, salt and dried chilies) in the bustling mercados of Oaxaca and Puebla. Or nutty *escamoles* (ant larvae)—often called "Mexican caviar" due to its rarity and richness—on the menu at traditional restaurants in Veracruz and Hidalgo.

29. Tras Horizonte

Brothers Pablo and Oso Campos launched the Tacos Kokopelli street cart in 2010 and have since expanded to their new home at Tras Horizonte. Devotees of Kokopelli's "modern tacos" can rest easy—they're still serving the greatest hits here. The Kraken is a standout, featuring grilled octopus marinated in Mexican-style pesto and topped with fresh avocado. Tacos are served with a medley of homemade salsas, including pumpkin seed, guava and habanero.

TIJUANA/CENTRAL

What to order:
The Kraken taco

Location:
Río Colorado 9680
Marron
22015 Tijuana

Hours:
Thu-Sat: 1 p.m. - 10 p.m.
Sun & Wed: 1 p.m. - 8 p.m.
Closed Mon & Tue

Phone:
+52 664 622 5062

In Tijuana, a selection of the 500+ edible insects that crawl, fly and burrow their way through Mexico can be found in markets and restaurants throughout the city. At restaurant Cien Años in the Zona Rio neighborhood, chef José Sparza serves a tasting menu of insects prepared vis-a-vis traditional methods. "Like fruits and vegetables, edible insects are seasonal," says the chef. "That means chapulines from August until December and *gusanos de maguey* (worms from the leaves of the maguey plant) in July and August."

Sparza serves his insects as tacos tucked into warm, house-made tortillas of white, yellow and blue heirloom corn. Tacos of escamoles, chapulines, *chicatanas* (flying ants from Oaxaca) and gusanos de maguey are featured during the tasting, as well as *chinicuiles*. These minuscule red worms reside in the roots of agave cultivated for tequila and mezcal and are unearthed en masse, fried on a comal until crispy, seasoned with salt and lime and often garnished with a dollop of guacamole.

Chef José Sparza oversees the preparation of escamoles (ant larvae) at Cien Años, Tijuana

TIJUANA/EAST

1. Aqui es Texcoco
2. Birria "Si"
3. La Carreta Taco Shop
4. La Única de Culiacán
5. Mariscos D'Tocho
6. Mariscos El Angel
7. Mariscos El Mazateño
8. Mariscos y Cahuamanta Obregón
9. Taco-n-Todo
10. Tacos de Cabeza (sin nombre)
11. Tacos El Dorado
12. Tacos El Gallito
13. Tacos El Primo
14. Xolotacos

VIEW ON GOOGLE MAPS

UNITED STATES
MEXICO

Otay Mesa Border Crossing

Aeropuerto
International
de Tijuana

Nueva Tijuana

Otay Vista

Rio Tijuana

1. Aqui es Texcoco

Aqui es Texcoco in Tijuana's Otay area is the original spot that spawned the Chula Vista eatery just across the border. Much like its northern counterpart, lamb barbacoa is the star of the menu here. However, a key difference lies in the preparation: the lamb is wrapped in maguey leaves and pit-roasted overnight south of the border. Barbacoa purists believe this preparation imparts its distinct flavor. Top with the dense, deeply-rich and flavorful salsa borracha.

TIJUANA/EAST

What to order:
Lamb barbacoa tacos

Location:
Instituto Politécnico Nacional
Campos Deportivos
22510 Tijuana

Hours:
Fri-Sun: 7 a.m. - 2 p.m.
Closed Mon-Thu

Phone:
+52 664 623 2800

2. Birria "Si"

Birria "Si" is a departure from the typical Jalisco-style birria de res offered in the city. The specialty here is Poblano-style spiced, stewed and shredded beef, notable for its pronounced flavor of cumin and cinnamon. The slightly nutty and peppery undertones of the spices enhance the broth's complexity, giving the birria a robust depth of flavor. Just say "si" when asked "¿con todo?", and onions, cilantro and shredded cabbage—another hallmark of the Poblano style—are added.

What to order:
Birria de res taco

Location:
Belisario Domínguez
y o C. 11 329
Libertad
22400 Tijuana

Hours:
Mon, Wed-Sat: 6 a.m. - 7:30 p.m.
Sun & Tue: 6 a.m. - 4 p.m.
Cash Only

Phone:
+52 664 234 0887

3. La Carreta Taco Shop

Baja California is renowned for its fish, adobada and carne asada tacos and chef Robert Mendoza at La Carreta puts a creative spin on these classics. An example is the shrimp al pastor. Buttery Baja shrimp are marinated in a blend of chiles, vinegar, achiote and citrus, then grilled and topped with pineapple, pickled red onion and cilantro. The beet, cilantro and blue corn tortillas add an extra layer of vibrancy and flavor.

What to order:
Shrimp al pastor taco

Location:
Diego Rivera 2347
Zona Rio
22010 Tijuana, Baja

Hours:
Mon-Thu: 12 p.m. - 9 p.m.
Fri-Sat: 12 p.m. - 10:30 p.m.
Closed Sun

Phone:
+52 664 387 2301

Birria de res taco with shredded cabbage at Birria "Si", Tijuana

The Legend of the Baja California-Style Fish Taco

Baja-style fish taco at El Prieto Food Truck, San Diego

Fish taco aficionados debate whether the first fillet was battered and fried in Ensenada or San Felipe, Baja California. Yet most agree that it was Japanese fishermen who immigrated to the region in the 1950s and 60s who first concocted one of the region's most iconic seafood specialties. They dipped fillets from the day's catch in tempura batter, fried them in *manteca*—typically pork fat—wrapped them in readily-available corn tortillas and finished the tacos with a squeeze of lime, shredded cabbage, pico de gallo, a splash of salsa and a dollop of crema. This provided a filling meal that satisfied their appetites after a long day on the water.

Ensenada's Tacos El Fénix, established in 1970, claims to have been the first to commercially popularize the fish taco, now a staple throughout the Baja peninsula and beyond. Rubio's Fish Tacos introduced the fried fish taco to San Diego after its founder had his first taste of one at a small stand in San Felipe on the Sea of Cortez's northern coast. As with many culinary trends, the fish taco eventually emigrated from Southern California to become popular across the U.S.

In Ensenada, the choice of fish is usually shark—*angelito*, *cazón* (dogfish) or mako. In San Diego, far too many taco shops use tilapia or *swai*—farmed fish sold en masse without much thought given to quality or taste. Though many taquerias in America's finest city insist on a higher-quality catch. At La Corriente in La Jolla, locally-sourced red snapper is the highlight of their delectable Ensenada-style fish taco. Fuego Marino, a popular food truck, uses locally-caught halibut. Very good to excellent Baja-style fish tacos can also be found at El Prieto Food Truck, Kiko's Place Seafood, El Viejón Seafood, Fish Guts, SeaTaco and Oscar's Mexican Seafood.

When in Baja California, one doesn't need to go all the way to Ensenada for an authentic Baja California fish taco. Mariscos stands and seafood restaurants, such as Tijuana's Mariscos el Angel, fry and serve their delectable versions of the dish to the city's fish taco faithful.

4. La Única de Culiacán

La Única de Culiacán is the go-to spot for Tijuanenses craving Sinaloa-style cabeza. Their *caldos* (soups) and tacos highlight tender cuts like cachete, lengua, maciza and ojos. For a unique twist, try a corn tortilla quesadilla slathered in asientos, the savory fried dregs left in the lard at the bottom of the pots used for cooking cabeza. With several locations around town, it's a must-visit for traditional flavors.

TIJUANA/EAST

What to order:
Cabeza tacos

Location:
Ca. del Tecnológico 14031
Universidad Otay
22427 Tijuana

Hours:
Daily: 7 a.m. - 2 p.m.

Phone:
+52 664 624 1655

5. Mariscos D'Tocho

This family-run truck boasts an array of seafood tacos and tantalizing mariscos. A popular order is the enchilado shrimp taco—drenched in generous dollops of crema and salsa. The taco delivers a fiery flavor explosion that begs for a refreshing sip of one of the house-made aguas frescas. For a twist, dive into the smoked marlin taco, where the smoky fish undergoes a brief fry, marrying its savory allure with a delightful crunch.

What to order:
Enchilado shrimp taco

Location:
Jose Vazconcelos
y Salvador Lobo
Modulo 1
22435 Tijuana

Hours:
Thu-Sun: 10:30 a.m. - 5:30 p.m.
Closed Mon-Wed

Phone:
+52 664 763 2700

6. Mariscos El Angel

One doesn't need to go all the way to Ensenada for an authentic Baja-style fish taco. Tijuana's Mariscos El Angel batters and fries their flaky fillets to golden perfection and finishes them with the requisite toppings—cabbage, crema and pico de gallo. An array of house-made and bottled salsas are available to add a splash of heat. The crunchy battered shrimp is another winning taco here. They also serve a full menu of Mexican mariscos such as ceviches, cocteles and aguachiles.

What to order:
Fried fish taco

Location:
De las Lomas 485
Colonia Buena Vista
22415 Tijuana

Hours:
Mon-Wed: 9 a.m. - 4 p.m.
Fri-Sun: 9 a.m. - 4 p.m.
Closed Thu

7. Mariscos El Mazateño

TIJUANA/EAST

Mariscos El Mazateño has a well-earned reputation as THE spot for the best Sinaloan-style seafood tacos in Tijuana. The crowd of diners seated at this open-air restaurant is testament to its popularity. The *El Perrón* taco combines generous amounts of flavorful grilled Baja shrimp and crunchy fried red snapper heaped into two warm, just-made flour tortillas. Melted Oaxacan cheese finishes the taco and is a welcome complement.

What to order:
El Perrón taco

Location:
Calz. del Tecnológico 473
Tomas Aquino
22414 Tijuana

Hours:
Daily: 8 a.m. - 7 p.m.

Phone:
+52 664 607 1377

8. Mariscos y Cahuamanta Obregón

This lively, colorfully-decorated fonda offers a taste of the Sonoran coast. The specialty here is the hearty, namesake stew of manta ray in vegetables and broth, served by the bowl or as tacos. Order it with aleta and gelatinous tuna fin is added, providing balance with the firm ray meat. Cahuamanta tacos are finished with shredded cabbage, red onions, celery and tomatoes and can be drizzled with one of the very good house-made salsas.

What to order:
Cahuamanta and aleta taco

Location:
Av. Ferrocarril 1340
Libertad
22400 Tijuana

Hours:
Daily: 7:30 a.m. - 8 p.m.

Phone:
+52 664 914 5125

9. Taco-n-Todo

Tijuana's beloved Taco-n-Todo specializes in carne asada, the crown jewel being the *taco de costilla*. This rib meat taco comes with the bone on the side, inviting one to gnaw and savor every bite of the tender, well-seasoned meat. It's served on a warm flour tortilla and topped with pickled red onions and a tangy salsa roja. There are several of these popular carts located throughout Tijuana.

What to order:
Costilla de res (beef rib) taco

Location:
Blvd. Lázaro Cárdenas 602
Otay Constituyentes
22457 Tijuana

Hours:
Tue-Sun: 1:30 p.m. - 11 p.m.
Closed Mon

Phone:
+52 664 305 7977

Cahuamanta and aleta taco at Mariscos y Cahuamanta Obregón, Tijuana

La Libertad: Timeless Tacos in Tijuana's Oldest Neighborhood

Steaming cabeza at Tacos de Cabeza (sin nombre) cart in Colonia Libertad

Located just a stone's throw from the border, Tijuana's Colonia Libertad holds a colorful past that's as steeped in flavor as the tacos on offer there. Established in the early 20th century, "La Libertad" was one of Tijuana's first formal settlements, initially populated by migrants seeking opportunities in the burgeoning border town. The area's name, which translates to "Freedom Colony," reflects the aspirations of its early inhabitants, who sought a new beginning and the freedom to forge a better life.

The neighborhood quickly grew, characterized by its vibrant streets and a sense of community resilience. Over the decades, Colonia Libertad became a melting pot of cultures and traditions, with each wave of new residents adding their unique flavor to the community. This rich tapestry of influences is most deliciously evident in the local cuisine.

10. Tacos de Cabeza (sin nombre)

The low-key Tacos de Cabeza *sin nombre* (no name)—in operation for over 45 years in Tijuana's colonia Libertad—offers some of the finest cabeza in Tijuana. One can order tacos of succulent cabeza, tender cachete, luscious lengua, unctuous ojos or creamy sesos. Try a campechano to savor a delightful combination of these flavors. There's a small seating area, but tacos are best ordered and enjoyed one at a time while standing at the cart.

What to order:
Taco campechano of cachete and sesos

Location:
Callejon José María Pino Suárez 11980
Buena Vista, Libertad
22400 Tijuana

Hours:
Mon-Sat: 3 p.m. - 9 p.m. (or when sold out)
Closed Sun
Cash only

By the mid-20th century, La Libertad had cemented its reputation as a culinary hotspot, drawing food enthusiasts from both sides of the border. The area became synonymous with tacos, a testament to the community's diverse regional Mexican culinary heritage. Families who settled in the neighborhood brought with them their hometown recipes and techniques—often passed down through generations—resulting in a unique fusion of flavors and styles.

Today, some of the most beloved taco stands in Colonia Libertad have been offering their delectable tacos and antojitos for over 40 years. These establishments are more than just places to eat; they are local institutions. Stands like Tacos de Cabeza *sin nombre* (no name) have become landmarks, renowned for their dedication to quality and tradition.

Mariscos y Cahuamanta Obregón, Colonia Libertad

Over the years, a number of stands and fondas launched in the colonia, each specializing in regional tacos. From Poblano-style birria de res at Birria "Si", to tacos of *cahuamanta* (manta ray stew) from Sonora at Mariscos y Cahuamanta Obregón, Colonia Libertad is a veritable cornucopia of taco styles.

11. Tacos El Dorado

Tacos El Dorado, with five locations across Tijuana, is an overwhelmingly-popular choice for birria de res. The original location in Otay Mesa stands out as one of the best. Specializing exclusively in birria de res, they offer it in all its varied and delectable forms: traditional tacos, a cheesy quesabirria in a large flour tortilla or in a bowl topped with cilantro and onions. Add a splash of salsa roja to finish the taco.

What to order:
Quesabirria maíz taco

Location:
Campos Deportivos
Otay Mesa
22430 Tijuana

Hours:
Mon-Fri: 8 a.m. - 3 p.m.
Sat-Sun: 8 a.m. - 3:30 p.m.

Phone:
+52 664 359 8321

12. Tacos El Gallito

TIJUANA/EAST

Tacos El Gallito, a bustling cart stationed in front of Otay's famed Tacos el Gallo, can satisfy any taco craving. The perfectly-seasoned adobada, shaved straight into a house-made corn tortilla from a large trompo, is a highlight. The carne asada, a tender strip of steak topped with pinto beans and a paddle of grilled nopal cactus, is another standout. The suadero is marinated with a "secret recipe" redolent of citrus and herbs and is one of my favorites on either side of the border.

What to order:
Suadero taco

Location:
Lazaro Cardenas Blvd. 606
Otay Constituyentes
22457 Tijuana

Hours:
Mon-Thu: 1 p.m. - 2 a.m.
Fri-Sat: 11 a.m. - 2 a.m.
Sun: 11 a.m. - 12 a.m.

13. Tacos El Primo

This family-owned cart has specialized in New York strip steak tacos for over twenty years. A portion of whole, grilled steak is nestled in a supple tortilla and best ordered "con todo"—with avocado, onions, cilantro and beans. The burritos are a must-try: minced New York strip mingles with grilled chile California and melted mozzarella, all wrapped in a flour tortilla then toasted on the griddle. For the ultimate flavor, ask them to finish it with a link of tangy chorizo.

What to order:
Minced New York steak burrito

Location:
Callejon José María Pino Suárez
Buena Vista, Libertad
Tijuana 22400
Cash only

Hours:
Tue-Wed: 2 p.m. - 11 p.m.
Thu-Sat: 1:30 p.m. - 11:00 p.m.
Closed Sun-Mon
Cash only

14. Xolotacos

Xolotacos' rustic birria de res tacos are a local treasure and can be savored at any of their five Tijuana locations. In Otay, this bustling open-air fonda draws in-the-know taco connoisseurs. Here, they order tacos of birria de res dorado style—with crisped corn tortillas—alongside tuétano, chicharrones, tripas and more. For the ultimate birria de res taco, ask the taquero to add chicharrones and tripas. Don't forget to slather on the rich, incendiary salsa of chile de árbol.

What to order:
Birria taco with tuétano

Location:
Instituto Politécnico Nacional
Campos Deportivos
22430 Tijuana

Hours:
Mon-Sun: 7 a.m. - 2 p.m.
Sun: 7 a.m. - 7 p.m.
Cash only

New York strip steak taco at Tacos El Primo, Tijuana

TIJUANA/SOUTH

1. Carnitas El Tío Pepe
2. Carnitas Mr. Buches
3. Carreta Los Compadres
4. Erizo
5. Mariscos Los Cangrejos
6. Mariscos Walter
7. Tacos Alicia
8. Tacos de Birria Buchito
9. Tacos El Poblano
10. Tacos La Pasadita de la 20
11. Tacos Salseados

Chapultepec

El Rubi

VIEW ON GOOGLE MAPS

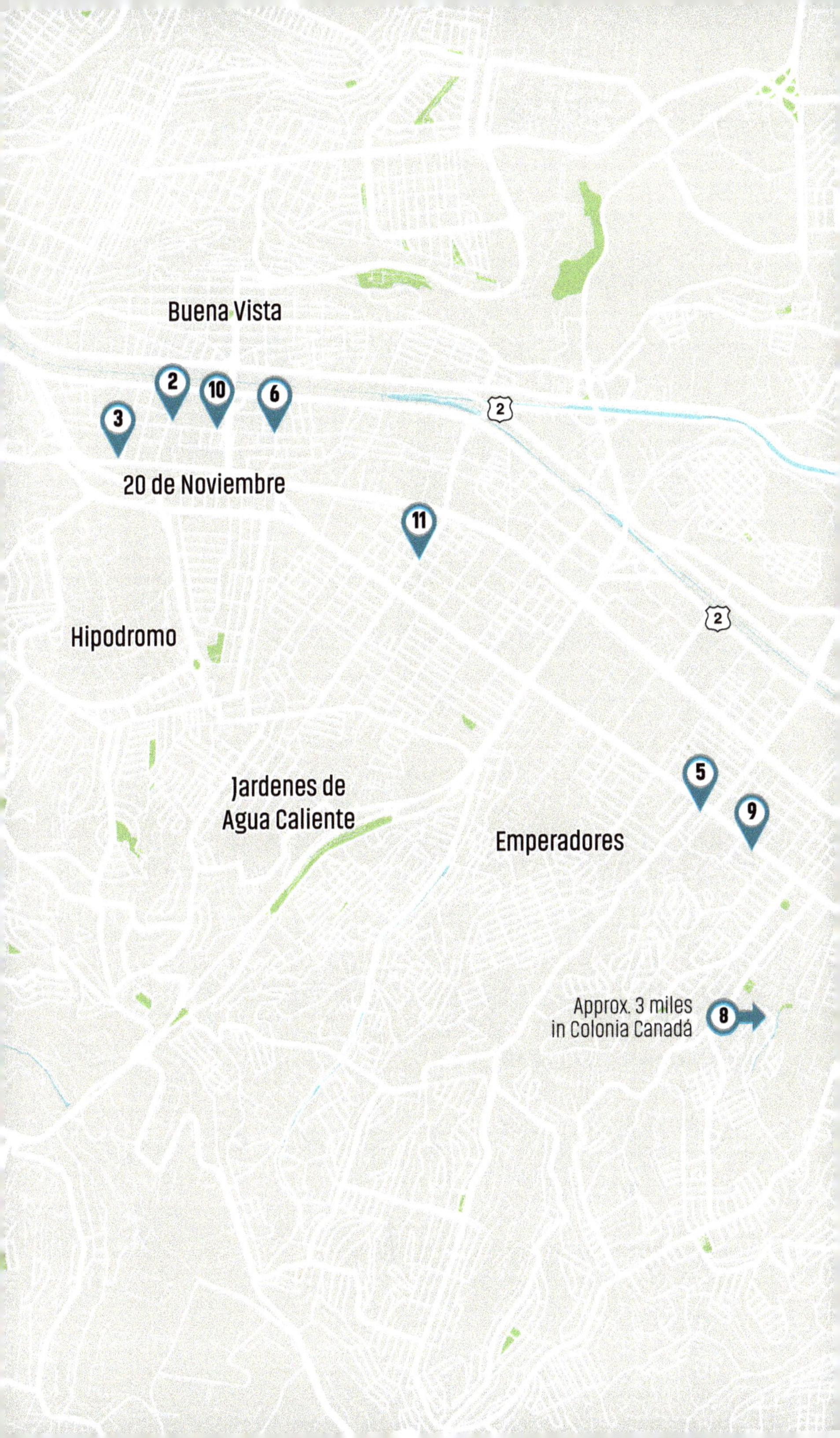

Buena Vista

2 10 6
3
20 de Noviembre

11

Hipodromo

Jardenes de
Agua Caliente

Emperadores

5
9

Approx. 3 miles
in Colonia Canadá 8

TIJUANA/SOUTH

1. Carnitas El Tío Pepe

Tío Pepe moved to Tijuana from Guadalajara in 1993 and began serving tortas ahogadas from a street cart in Zona Centro. He still offers tortas at his current space as well as a variety of other carnitas options. The *Chavez Especial* taco is crafted using surtida (mixed meats) heaped into a warm, house-made corn tortilla, which is then topped with melted cheese. Order it "con todo" and guacamole and a chunky pico de gallo are added.

What to order:
Chavez Especial taco

Location:
Gobernador García González #9925
Gabilondo
22045 Tijuana

Hours:
Wed-Mon: 7 a.m. - 6 p.m.
Closed Tue

Phone:
+52 664 972 9999

2. Carnitas Mr. Buches

For top-notch carnitas, head to Mr. Buche's in Colonia 20 de Noviembre. Tacos feature an array of tempting pork cuts; buche, *chamorro* (shank), costilla, maciza, *rabo* (tail) and more, each one heaped with fillings and toppings. The *La Puerquita* taco blends buche with maciza and is dressed with red and white onion, cilantro and tomatoes. Instead of a tortilla, it's presented in a savory, umami-rich round of griddled cheese.

What to order:
La Puerquita taco

Location:
Prol. Paseo de los Heroes 12650-12646
20 de Noviembre
22100 Tijuana

Hours:
Mon-Sat: 9 a.m. - 3 p.m.
Sun: 9 a.m. - 12:30 p.m.

Phone:
+52 664 389 8896

3. Carreta Los Compadres

Popular street cart Carreta Los Compadres offers a menu of tempting mariscos tacos. The camarón enchilado features plump Baja shrimp cooked on the griddle in a rich chipotle salsa with diced jalapeños. The *El Titan* is a meal unto itself, heaped with grilled shrimp, octopus and slabs of savory bacon and finished with red cabbage, tomatoes, crema and a generous portion of guacamole. These tacos are enormous—it's best to arrive with an appetite.

What to order:
El Titan taco

Location:
Av. 20 de Noviembre 12177
Calle Pacifico
20 de Noviembre
22100 Tijuana

Hours:
Daily: 9 a.m. - 3 p.m.

Phone:
+52 664 464 7154

El Titan taco at Carreta Los Compadres, Tijuana

Seafood tacos at Mariscos Walter, Tijuana

4. Erizo

Erizo, located in upscale Colonia Chapultepec, is chef Javier Plascencia's popular raw bar. Here, classic Baja California mariscos meet the chef's innovative culinary flair, especially the seafood tacos. The Ensenada-style fish taco features local fish, fried until satisfyingly crunchy. Specialties include a smoked tuna *machaca* taco and *birria de pescado*, which marries two Baja favorites by stewing locally-sourced fish with traditional birria seasonings.

TIJUANA/SOUTH

What to order:
Birria de pescado taco

Location:
Sonora 3808-2
Chapultepec
22020 Tijuana

Hours:
Sun-Wed: 11 a.m. - 8 p.m.
Thu-Sat: 11 a.m. - 9 p.m.

Phone:
+52 664 686 2895

5. Mariscos Los Cangrejos

Mariscos Los Cangrejos is housed in a ramshackle palapa beach shack located smack dab in the center of Tijuana's urban hustle. Kick back, relax and order from a variety of seafood tacos, including the delectable bacon-wrapped shrimp. Snappy, succulent grilled shrimp are wrapped in a strip of smoky, savory bacon. The taco is dressed with papaya, cabbage, cilantro and chipotle crema. This flawless taco pairs very well with a house-mixed michelada.

What to order:
Bacon-wrapped shrimp taco

Location:
Blvd. Gustavo Díaz Ordaz 1052
Infonavit La Mesa
22115 Tijuana

Hours:
Daily: 10 a.m. - 8 p.m.

Phone:
+52 664 154 3019

6. Mariscos Walter

Mariscos Walter is a paradise for seafood taco enthusiasts. This vibrant *marisquería* features a warm and inviting dining room where one can order from a tempting menu of tacos, from perfectly grilled pulpo with olives to the exquisite *De Klein* taco—which blends juicy, grilled shrimp with smoked marlin and tender aleta on a crispy corn tortilla. The menu also boasts an impressive selection of traditional mariscos, including ceviches, aguachiles and cocteles.

What to order:
De Klein taco

Location:
Prol Paseo de los Heroes 13051
20 de Noviembre
22100 Tijuana

Hours:
Mon-Sat: 8 a.m. - 6 p.m.
Closed Sun

Phone:
+52 664 378 5283

TIJUANA/SOUTH

7. Tacos Alicia

Tacos Alicia, off the beaten tourist path on Blvd. Fundadores, offers a wide variety of taco types, including savory carne asada, rich, fried suadero, lengua, cabeza and tripa. All tacos may be ordered on either house-made corn or flour tortillas. The adobada is exceptional due, in part, to the use of red onions: their sharp, yet subtle sweetness contrasts beautifully with the flavorfully-marinated pork.

What to order:
Adobada taco

Location:
Blvd. Fundadores S/N
Valle del Rubiseccion Lomas
22630 Tijuana

Hours:
Sun-Thu: 8 a.m. - 1:30 p.m.
Fri-Sat: 8 a.m. - 2 a.m.
Cash only

8. Tacos de Birria Buchito

Papada, pork jowl, is an ingredient rarely found in Tijuana taquerias. Tacos de Birria Buchito focuses solely on *birria de papada*—offering it as tacos, quesabirria, tostadas, stews and chicharrón in a rich, chunky salsa of chile de árbol. The pork is cooked on the griddle until it's flavorful and firm, then heaped onto a tortilla that's been dipped in consomé and fried until crispy. Top with the salsa chicharrón to impart additional heat and texture.

What to order:
Papada birria taco

Location:
3era Etapa de Rio Tijuana 22226
Canadá
22430 Tijuana

Hours:
Wed-Sat: 8 a.m. - 1:30 p.m.
Sun: 8 a.m. - 2 p.m.
Closed Mon-Tue
Cash only

Phone:
+52 664 175 2918

9. Tacos El Poblano

Imitators exist in the city, but the original Tacos El Poblano in Tijuana's La Mesa neighborhood—founded forty years ago—is considered to have some of the best carne asada in town. Their secret? Marinating the steak overnight and then grilling it over wood fire, imparting an irresistible smoky flavor. One can savor the carne asada in tacos, vampiros, mulitas and burritos. Their carne asada *tostadita* includes juicy morsels of grilled meat piled high on a small corn tortilla, fried on the grill until crisped.

What to order:
Carne asada tostadita

Location:
Blvd. Gustavo Díaz Ordaz 1177
Huertas 2da Secc.
22116 Tijuana

Hours:
Sun-Thu: 8 a.m. - 2 a.m.
Fri-Sat: 8 a.m. - 4 a.m.

Carne asada taco at Tacos Alicia, Tijuana

Tacos El Poblano, Tijuana

10. Tacos La Pasadita de la 20

Tacos La Pasadita is one of the busiest street cart operations in the city. The large staff tirelessly grill carne asada and jalapeños, shave adobada from two large trompos and craft thick corn tortillas from a massive mound of masa. The tortillas are the main attraction here; profoundly rich in corn flavor, they're loaded with asada, adobada—or both—and finished with a large dollop of guacamole. Arrive hungry—these tacos are easily twice the size of a typical TJ street taco.

What to order:
Carne asada taco

Location:
El Chorrito 12745
20 de Noviembre
22100 Tijuana
Cash only

Hours:
Daily: 6 p.m. - 12 a.m.

Tacos La Pasadita de la 20, Tijuana

11. Tacos Salseados

Tacos Salseados is widely acknowledged to have invented the *quesotaco*, where a crispy, fried cheese shell replaces the typical tortilla. A standout dish is the smoked marlin quesotaco, adorned with plump, grilled shrimp atop thinly-shaved slices of rare NY strip steak. The taco is finished with velvety avocado and drizzled with a rich, smoky chipotle salsa. This taqueria is so popular in the neighborhood, it's simply known as "La Ermita", the street on which it's located.

TIJUANA/SOUTH

What to order:
Surf and turf quesotaco

Location:
Calz. Ermita Norte 30
Santa Cruz
22105 Tijuana

Hours:
Wed-Mon: 1 p.m. - 11 p.m.
Closed Tue
Cash only

Phone:
+52 664 608 1744

TIJUANA/WEST

1. Mariscos Ruben's y Charlie's
2. Mariscos Tito's
3. Mr. Pollo Tacos de Pollo
4. Tacos Aaron
5. Tacos El Che
6. Tacos El Francés

VIEW ON GOOGLE MAPS

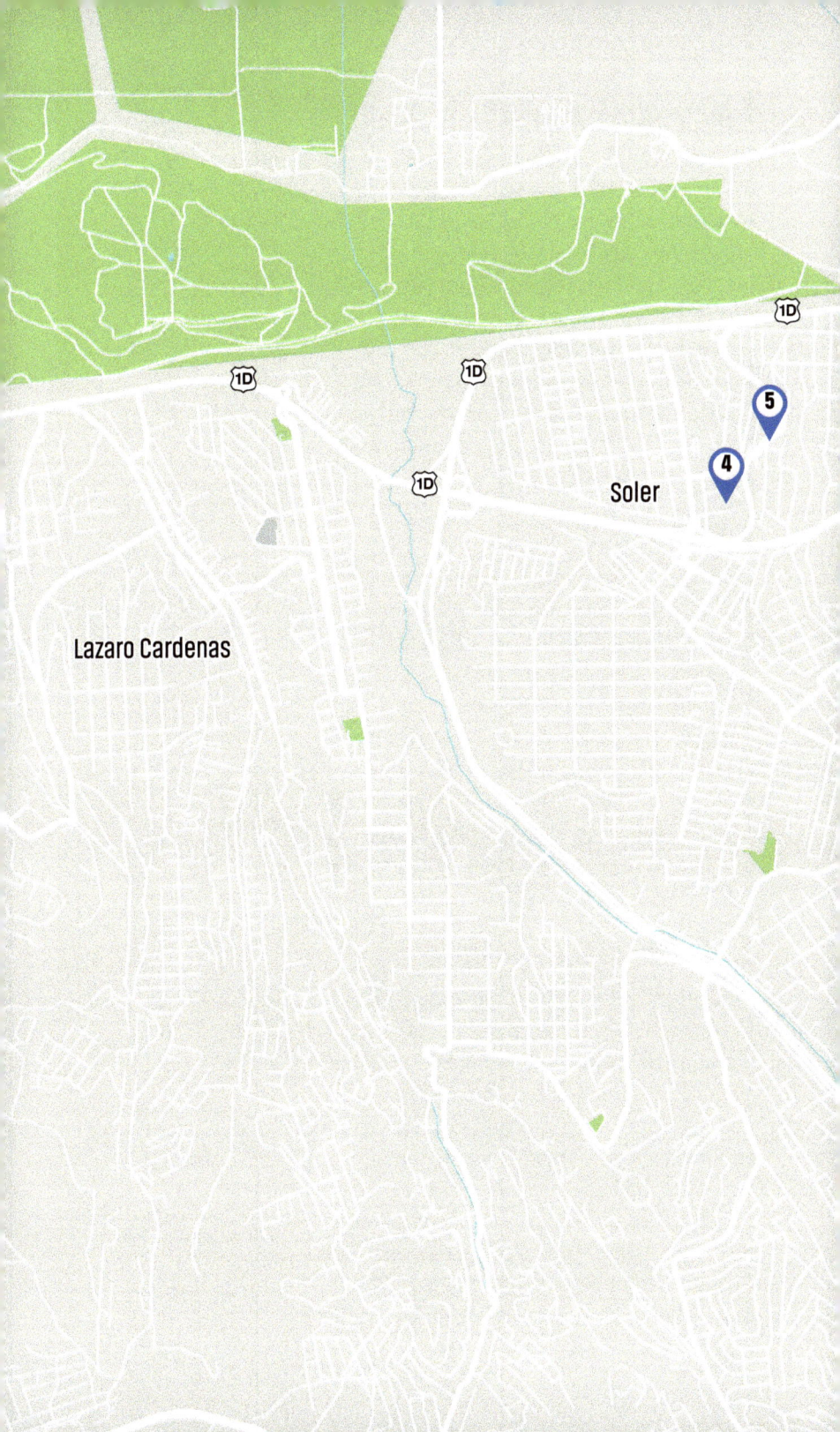

1. Mariscos Ruben's y Charlie's

Tijuana's cherished Mariscos Ruben, a fixture in Zona Rio for nearly thirty years, shuttered during the pandemic. But fans of their famous Sonoran-style seafood can rejoice—proprietor Mirtha Rodriguez now teams up with her son at Ruben's y Charlie's in Playas de Tijuana. Here, one can savor seafood tacos while soaking in the Pacific view and sipping a refreshing michelada. A must-try is the spicy enchilado taco, available with shrimp, octopus or both.

TIJUANA/WEST

What to order:
Octopus enchilado taco

Location:
Av. Del Pacifico 493
Costa
22667 Tijuana

Hours:
Daily: 8 a.m. - 10 p.m.

Phone:
+52 664 378 2421

2. Mariscos Tito's

Mariscos Tito's has been a cornerstone of Tijuana's seafood scene since 1969, boasting five locations across the city. This beloved institution's menu lists a bounty of mariscos—from aguachiles to *pescado zarandeado* (Sinaloa-style grilled fish). They also offer over two dozen tacos. The *trucha* taco is a standout—trout, fried milanesa style, is combined with shrimp and griddled cheese and finished with avocado and a smoky chipotle crema—all served on a flour tortilla.

What to order:
Trucha taco

Location:
Islas Coronado 204
Coronado
Playas de Tijuana
22500 Tijuana

Hours:
Daily: 10 a.m. - 9 p.m.

Phone:
+52 664 630 0307

3. Mr. Pollo Tacos de Pollo

This bright yellow wood-constructed cart in Playas de Tijuana specializes in one thing, and they do it exceptionally well. Coated in a blend of "secret" spices, roasted then expertly finished on a charcoal grill, the chicken here is incomparable. Ask the taquero to chop it in larger morsels to savor every smoky, spice-infused bite. The *quesapollo*, featuring melted cheese on a flour tortilla, is a standout. Or, for a satisfying crunch, try it as a tostada—each bite is pure, juicy delight.

What to order:
Tostada de pollo

Location:
Parque Azteca Nte.
Playas de Tijuana
Jardines del Sol
22505 Tijuana

Hours:
Mon-Sat: 11 a.m. - 11 p.m.
Sun: 12 p.m. - 11 p.m.

Phone:
+52 664 588 6101

Mr. Pollo Tacos de Pollo, Playas de Tijuana

Clockwise from top left: Blue Azul bacon-wrapped shrimp, trucha (trout), gobernador and Baja-style battered fish tacos at Mariscos Tito's, Tijuana.

Tripas and suadero tacos at Tacos El Ché, Tijuana

4. Tacos Aaron

The Tacos Aaron food truck has specialized in tacos de guisados for over 20 years. The standout is the *chicharrón en salsa verde*. It features hearty chunks of fried pork skin, still clinging to tender meat, all bathed in a zesty, tomatillo-based salsa verde and finished with tangy, pickled red onions. There are multiple trucks around Tijuana, but the one in Soler is the original and considered the best.

TIJUANA/WEST

What to order:
Chicharrón en salsa verde taco

Location:
Independencia 4500
Soler
22530 Tijuana

Hours:
Daily: 7 a.m. - 2:30 p.m.
Cash only

Phone:
+52 664 550 1339

5. Tacos El Che

Tacos El Che, located in Colonia Alemán, is off the beaten TJ taco path, but well worth the diversion. The luscious, fatty suadero, redolent of lemon and just the right amount of salt, may be the best in the city. Tripas are expertly fried and served "wet" or crunchy, depending on one's taste. The taqueros make a show of splashing a bit of the grease from the griddle onto the heating element behind the spit of adobada, creating an impressive flame and charring the pork to perfection.

What to order:
Suadero taco

Location:
Via Internacional 52
Alemán
22050 Tijuana

Hours:
Sun-Thu: 3 p.m. - 11:30 p.m.
Fri-Sat: 3 p.m. - 1 a.m.

6. Tacos El Francés

For over fifty years, Tacos El Francés has been a cherished institution among Tijuanenses, and it's easy to see why. Their suadero and tripas, steeped in a marinade rich with chiles and spices, deliver a tangy, vibrant flavor. The adobada and carne asada are finished with creamy guacamole. A splash of the fiery red salsa takes it over the top. Don't miss their house-made corn tortillas—tender, warm and fresh off the griddle. Simply put, these are some of the best tacos in Tijuana.

What to order:
Suadero taco

Location:
Playas de Tijuana 1442
Costa de Oro
22506 Tijuana

Hours:
Mon-Thu: 3 p.m. - 11 p.m.
Fri-Sat: 2 p.m. - 12 a.m.
Closed Sun

Tacos El Francés, Tijuana

GLOSSARY

A

Achiote – A mild aromatic paste made of ground achiote seeds, often used in Yucatecan cooking

Adobada – A dish of Arab origin that became popular in Mexico during the 1960s. Pork is marinated in achiote, sour orange, chiles and spices, roasted on a revolving trompo (vertical spit), shaved off and served as an open taco—often with a chunk of pineapple cut from the fruit atop the trompo. Similar to al pastor in central Mexico.

Aguas frescas – Literally "fresh waters". Traditional Mexican drinks made with fresh fruits or vegetables pureed in a blender with sugar and water.

Aguacate – Avocado

Aguachile – Shrimp marinated in lime juice and chiles, typically serranos

Ahumado – Smoked

Al pastor – See adobada

Albondiga – Meatball. In Mexico, sometimes made with chicharrón as a binder instead of breadcrumbs.

Aleta – Tuna fin

Antojitos – Typically corn-based appetizers, essentially anything made with tortillas or *masa de maíz* (corn dough), eaten as a light meal or snack. Some of the most common antojitos in the Taco Megaregion are nachos, quesadillas, tamales, enchiladas and of course, tacos. Burritos are also considered an antojito, though they're made with wheat flour tortillas.

Apertivo – A post-dinner drink, typically mezcal or tequila in Mexico

Arrachera – Thinly sliced and seasoned skirt steak

Asadero – An eatery specializing in roasted meats

Asado – Roasted

Asientos – Savory fried dregs left in the lard at the bottom of the pots used for cooking cabeza, typically served on a quesadilla made with a corn tortilla

Atún – Tuna

B

Barbacoa – Usually sheep or goat, baked in a pit in maguey leaves, and served as tacos. In San Diego, it's typically made in a commercial roaster, due to stringent restaurant codes. Common in central Mexico as a fiesta or wedding dish.

Birria – A spicy stew usually made with goat or mutton, often served during festive periods such as Christmas, New Year's Eve and at weddings. Originally from Jalisco, it's served with tortillas, onion, cilantro, lime, salsa and typically, with a bowl of its own broth as accompaniment.

Birria de res – Beef birria

Birrieria – An eatery specializing in birria

Borrego – Lamb

Buche – Pork stomach

Burrito – Ingredients and toppings rolled in a wheat flour tortilla. Common in northern Mexico and an overwhelmingly popular order in the Taco Megaregion. In Mexico, burritos are typically small, whereas in San Diego, they are as big as one's forearm.

C

Cabeza de res – Beef head

Cachete de res – Beef cheek

Cahuamanta – A hearty Sonoran stew of manta ray, shrimp and vegetables in a seasoned broth

California burrito – A large burrito filled with carne asada, rice, beans, guacamole and French fries. It originated in San Diego and is a popular order at the city's taco shops.

Callo de hacha – Jumbo scallops

Camarones – Shrimp

Camarón capeado – Battered and fried shrimp

Campechano – A taco of mixed meats or ingredients

Cangrejo – Crab (also called jaiba)

Carne – Meat, commonly used to refer to beef

Carne asada – Marinated then grilled, or griddled beef, typically skirt steak, though other cuts are used throughout the Taco Megaregion

Carne deshebrada – Shredded beef in red sauce

Carnitas – Pork boiled, then fried in its own fat. Taquerias specializing in carnitas usually offer nearly every part of the pig from the cheeks to the tail.

Cebolla – Onion

Cecina – Marinated, thinly-pounded, air-dried pork

Cerdo – Pork (also puerco)

Cerveza – Beer (*oscura* is dark, *clara*, light)

Cerveza artesanal – Craft beer made by small breweries. San Diego and Tijuana are both considered craft beer capitals in their respective countries.

Ceviche – Seafood that's been "cooked" by marinating in citrus juice; there are many regional variations, but the best is found on the Pacific coast, including Baja California.

Chile relleno – Chile stuffed with cheese and other ingredients, then battered and fried

Chivo – Goat

Chamorro – A roasted portion of beef or pork leg

Chapulines – Grasshoppers, eaten deep fried and seasoned with salt, citrus, garlic and chile flakes

Chicatanas – Edible flying ants from Oaxaca

Chicharrón – Pork skin, eaten deep fried or in stews

Chilaquiles – Fried tortilla chips cooked in crema and salsa until soft

Chimichurri – An Argentinian sauce made of finely-chopped flat leaf parsley, minced garlic, olive oil, oregano, red pepper flakes and red wine vinegar. Sometimes offered as a carne asada taco topping alongside the typical salsas.

Choriqueso – Chorizo combined with melted cheese, often served as a taco

Chorizo – Pork or beef sausage

Chorizo verde – Pork or beef sausage made green by the addition of fresh chiles, parsley and garlic, which are puréed and mixed into ground pork along with spices and a tangy dose of sherry vinegar.

Cilantro – Coriander. One of the most common meat taco toppings.

Cochinita pibil – Yucatecan shredded pork, cooked with achiote, sour orange, chiles and spices

Cocina – Kitchen

Coctel – Mexican seafood cocktail

Comal – A metal or ceramic plate on which tortillas are cooked. Can also refer to the deep concave fryer used to cook suadero and tripas at taquerias.

Comida (lunch) – This is the main meal of the day for most Mexicans and is usually not eaten before 2 p.m.

Con todo – With everything

Conejo – Rabbit

Consomé – Broth

Costillas – Beef or pork ribs

Cotija – A crumbly Mexican cheese

Crema – Similar to sour cream, though usually lighter in consistency

Cueritos – Pork skin

D

Digestivo – a pre-dinner drink, typically mezcal or tequila in Mexico

Dorados – A taco in a corn tortilla fried on the griddle until "golden" as the name implies. Many taquerias offer this as an option, particularly for birria de res tacos, where the tortilla is first dipped in consomé before frying.

E

Elote – Grilled Mexican-style corn on the cob, slathered with mayonnaise and dressed with cotija cheese, chiles, garlic, cilantro and lime

Enchilado – A preparation, commonly shrimp, of ingredients in a spicy red chile stew

Escamoles – Edible ant larvae

F

Frijoles de olla – Stewed pinto beans made with onion and garlic

Frito – Fried

G

Gobernador – Taco made of shrimp with melted cheese, served on a toasted flour tortilla, originally made for the governor of Sinaloa, Mexico, in the 1990s

Guacamole – Made with avocado mashed with tomato, onion, garlic and seasoning

Guisados – Stews

Gusano de maguey – An edible worm that lives in the maguey cactus

H

Harina – Flour

Hongos – Mushrooms

Horchata – Pronounced "orCHATa". A sweet drink usually made from rice.

Huarache – A large, thick tortilla topped with meat or cheese; so-called because it is the size and shape of a shoe.

Huevos – Eggs

Huitlacoche – Black corn fungus with a subtle mushroom taste

J

Jaca – Jackfruit

Jaiba – Crab

Jamaica – Pronounced "haMIKEa". A popular agua fresca made of hibiscus.

Jurel – Yellowtail, a fish common to the San Diego-Tijuana region and member of the Jack family.

L

Labia de res – Beef lips

Langosta – Lobster

Lengua de res – Beef tongue

Limón – Green lime

Limón amarillo – Lemon

M

Machaca – Dried beef, typical of northern Mexico

Maciza – Lean cuts of pork carnitas

Maíz – Corn

Manteca – Lard

Mariscada – A combination of seafood, a seafood feast

Mariscos – Seafood, shellfish

Masa – Corn dough

Menuderia – An eatery specializing in menudo

Menudo – Tripe stew, popular as a hangover remedy

Mezcal – A spirit made from the piña (core) of various maguey plants, native to central and southern Mexico.

Michelada – A classic Mexican cocktail with beer, Clamato juice, lime, Worcestershire and hot sauce. Served in a glass rimmed with *chamoy*.

Milanesa – Pounded, breaded and fried pork, beef or chicken

Molcajete – Traditional mortar made of volcanic stone

Mole – A sauce containing many ingredients such as herbs, chiles, vegetables and thickened with seeds such as pepita, sesame or peanut. Some dark moles contain a small amount of chocolate, but calling mole a "chocolate sauce" is erroneous.

Moranga – Mexican blood sausage

Mulita – A taco variation where fillings and toppings are sandwiched between two lightly cooked tortillas and finished with melted cheese. Sometimes referred to as a *mula*.

N

Nachos – A Tex Mex concoction of tortilla chips and melted cheese, commonly topped with pickled jalapeño chiles

Nervio – Beef tendon

Nopales – Cactus paddles eaten as a vegetable throughout Mexico. Found at taquerias where they're often grilled and served atop a whole cut of carne asada. Nopalitos, cactus salad, can be found at taquerias as a topping, particularly those that specialize in tacos varios (guisados).

O

Ojos – Eyes. Beef eye ligament is commonly used as a taco filling in Mexico.

P

Papa – Potato

Pepino – Cucumber

Perrón – A Sonoran-style taco. Chopped arrachera is dressed with onion, cilantro, guacamole, melted cheese and pinto beans and served on a large flour tortilla.

Pescado – Fish

Pescado capeado – Battered and fried fish

Picadillo – Chopped meat with tomatoes and chili, often with raisins or nuts, used as filling for chiles or tacos

Picaña – Fatty beef sirloin cap

Picante – Hot, spicy

Pico de gallo – A salsa of fresh tomato, onion, chile, cilantro and lime. Also referred to as salsa Mexicana or salsa bandera.

Pierna – Leg (of pork or lamb when referring to food)

Piña – Pineapple

Plancha – Griddle

Pollo – Chicken

Puerco – Pork, pig

Pulpo – Octopus

Q

Quesabirria – A birria taco, commonly beef, topped with melted cheese and fried on the griddle to give the tortilla a crispy texture.

Quesadillas – Most commonly, a tortilla filled with cheese, folded and cooked on a round metal griddle. Sometimes they are deep-fried. In Tijuana, both corn and flour tortillas are used, but in San Diego—as well as throughout the U.S.—flour is more common.

Queso – Cheese

Queso Oaxaqueño – String cheese

Quesotaco – A taco where a round of melted, griddled cheese is used in place of a corn or flour tortilla. Commonly referred to as a "keto taco" in health-conscious San Diego.

R

Rábano – Radish

Res – Beef

Rolled tacos – A type of taco where corn tortillas are rolled, fried until crispy and filled with ingredients. They're usually dressed with sour cream, guacamole, lettuce and finely-shredded cheddar cheese.

S

Sal – Salt

Salsa – Sauce

Salsa macha – A salsa made with a variety of dried peppers, garlic, nuts and oil

Salsa molcajete – Salsa of roasted chiles and vegetables, blended in a molcajete

Salsa picante – Hot sauce

Salsa roja – Red salsa, made with tomato and chiles, or just chiles. Chiles de árbol are common for salsa roja in the Taco Megaregion.

Salsa tatemada – Salsa of chiles and vegetables roasted until charred, which infuses it with a rich, smoky flavor

Salsa verde – Green salsa made with tomatillos and fresh chiles, commonly jalapeño or serrano

Sandía – Watermelon

Sesos – Brains

Sopes – Small discs of corn masa are fried and then topped with beans, chicken, chorizo—the variety is endless. Often served as appetizers in restaurants or at street stalls.

Soyrizo – Vegan chorizo made with soybeans

Street tacos – Generally used as a catch-all term for smaller meat-based tacos in the U.S. In Mexico, tacos prepared and served on the street.

Suadero – A smooth Mexican cut of beef, located near the brisket—fried and served as tacos. Often called "rose meat" due to its pink coloration.

Surtido – Mixed cuts of pork carnitas

T

Tacos – A soft or fried corn or flour tortilla with fillings, toppings and salsa, folded or rolled and eaten with the hands. Available with a nearly infinite combination of fillings. Beloved on both sides of the U.S.-Mexico border as well as around the world.

Tacos de canasta – Steamed tacos are served from a basket and covered in a damp cloth. They're very popular in Mexico City. *Tacos a vapor* are the nearest equivalent in the Taco Megaregion.

Tamales – (Singular "*tamal*") Tamales vary from region to region and are found all over Latin America, with different names, but the basic idea is ground corn wrapped in its husk (usually corn) and steamed for hours. The masa (corn dough) is mixed with lard and usually contains a small amount of filling: chicken or pork with red sauce, green sauce, or mole, or strips of chili Poblano with cheese are the most common.

Tatemado – Burnt. A technique used in Mexican cuisine where ingredients like meats, chiles, vegetables and tortillas are cooked until burnt. In Mexico, ash is commonly used as an ingredient for salsas and other recipes.

Taqueria – An establishment serving tacos

Taquear – A taco crawl

Taquero – A cook specializing in tacos

Tasajo – Marinated, thinly-pounded, air-dried beef

Tequila – A spirit made from the piña (core) of blue Weber agave, solely from the state of Jalisco

Tilapia – A white fish, usually farmed. Many San Diego taquerias make their battered and fried fish tacos using this inexpensive variety, typically considered of low quality.

TJ – Tijuana. An acronym used by many living in the Megaregion.

Tlayuda – Corn tortilla "flatbread" with beans, lard, cheese, tomatoes and meat

Tortas – Mexico´s version of the sandwich, supposedly invented by an Italian immigrant at the turn of the 20th century, is a soft roll (*bolillo*) with a wide range of ingredients. A few popular choices are Cuban (with ham), milanesa, *pierna* (roast pork) and choriqueso, but the variety is endless. Garnishes include tomato, onion, avocado, cheese, lettuce, mayonnaise and jalapeño or chipotle chiles.

Torta ahogada – A torta "drowned" in a tomato and chile-based red sauce. From the Mexican state of Jalisco.

Tortillas – The cornerstone of Mexican cuisine. The ubiquitous tortilla—a staple since the pre-Hispanic era—is essentially ground corn, softened with cal (chemical lime), called nixtamal, flattened into a disc and cooked on a griddle. Flour tortillas are common in the north and found throughout the Taco Megaregion. Tortillas are the basic ingredient for tacos, enchiladas, tostadas, burritos, chilaquiles, flautas and a host of other Mexican dishes.

Tortilleria – A shop that makes tortillas

Tostada – A tortilla fried until crisp, then topped with various ingredients

Tripas de res – Beef small intestines

Trompo – A vertical spit used to roast adobada/al pastor

Tuétano – Bone marrow

V

Vampiro – A taco variation where fillings and toppings are sandwiched between two tortillas that are baked until crisped, then finished with melted cheese.

Vapor – Steam: Tacos a vapor are steamed and kept warm under a piece of damp cloth.

Varios – A Tijuana colloquialism for guisados. Tacos varios stands are common throughout the city.

ABOUT THE AUTHOR

The author with the taqueros at Carreta Los Compadres, Tijuana (Photo: Francisco Perez)

San Diego-based writer W. Scott Koenig has traveled throughout Mexico and Baja California since the mid 1990s. He founded AGringoInMexico.com in 2012 to report on Mexican cuisine, culture, destinations and events.

Scott is considered a key influencer in Baja California and San Diego. A Gringo in Mexico and its affiliated social channels are viewed by thousands in the U.S., Mexico and around the world daily.

Scott is author of the book *Seven Days in The Valle: Baja California's Wine Country Cuisine* and has written columns for *Dining Out San Diego*, *San Diego Red*, *Baja.com* and *Discover Baja*. He's also written features for several print and online publications, including *Newworlder*, *Destino Magazine* and *San Diego Magazine*.

Scott has curated and led public and private culinary tours of Baja California, including taco tours of Tijuana as a partner in Three Amigo Taco Tours. He has assisted with video productions in the region and has worked with Netflix, the Food Channel, the BBC, NPR, Unilever, Migrationology and the Culinary Institute of America.

Scott was co-host and co-producer of the YouTube show *Baja Window to the South*, has been featured on regional podcasts and is often called on to judge culinary competitions in San Diego and Baja California.

Scott has built a network of culinary professionals, business leaders, tourism officials, media agencies, writers and photographers in the San Diego-Baja California Megaregion.

Scott is the owner of Koenig Creative LLC in San Diego. He has 40 years of experience in marketing communications, creative direction and graphic design.

ALSO BY W. SCOTT KOENIG
Seven Days in the Valle: Baja California's Wine Country Cuisine

Seven Days in The Valle: Baja California's Wine Country Cuisine by W. Scott Koenig documents the lives, cuisine and restaurants of seven of Baja California's most talented chefs working in the Valle de Guadalupe, Mexico's main wine-producing region. In the last decade, the "Valle" has become a top international destination, widely renowned for its wine and food.

Through over 100 full-color photos, narrative and intimate interviews with the chefs, the book captures their passion for Baja California cuisine, their philosophies about the Valle (and its future) and reveals a bit of their souls in the process.

The book features: Drew Deckman of Deckman's en El Mogor; Esthela Martínez of La Cocina de Doña Esthela; Roberto Alcocer of Malva; Miguel Angel Guerrero of La Esperanza; Sheyla Alvarado of Traslomita; Diego Hernandez of Corazon de Tierra; and Javier Plascencia of Finca Altozano.

What the critics say about Seven Days in The Valle:

"This book has beautiful photos. It has great nuggets of insight from the chefs. At 56 pages it's easily digestible on your drive down there, which you should be making soon."
Troy Johnson, San Diego Magazine

"This beautifully-designed book should accompany every visitor to the Valle de Guadalupe, Baja California's wine country, offering essential tips and background information. Highly recommend!"
Nicholas Gilman, Good Food Mexico City

Order *Seven Days in the Valle: Baja California's Wine Country Cuisine* **domestically and internationally at Amazon.com, the Apple Bookstore and BN.com.**

Three Amigos Tijuana Taco Tours 2019:
Fernando Cuevas, Tours in Baja
W. Scott Koenig, Author, A Gringo in Mexico
Francisco (Paco) Perez, Aqui es Texcoco

www.ingramcontent.com/pod-product-compliance
Lightning Source LLC
Chambersburg PA
CBHW061737070526
44585CB00024B/2707